P9-CJL-463

TRANSFORMING A COLLEGE

TRANS-
FORMING A
COLLEGE

The Story of a
Little-Known College's
Strategic Climb to
National Distinction

Updated Edition

GEORGE KELLER

With a New Foreword by Leo M. Lambert

JOHNS HOPKINS UNIVERSITY PRESS
Baltimore

© 2004, 2014 Johns Hopkins University Press
All rights reserved. Published 2004, 2014
Printed in the United States of America on acid-free paper
2 4 6 8 9 7 5 3 1

Johns Hopkins University Press
2715 North Charles Street
Baltimore, Maryland 21218-4363
www.press.jhu.edu

The Library of Congress cataloged the earlier edition as follows:

Keller, George, 1928–
Transforming a college : the story of a little-known college's
strategic climb to national distinction / George Keller.
p.   cm.
Includes index.
ISBN 0-8018-7989-2 (hardcover : alk. paper)
1. Elon College—History. 2. Elon University—History. I. Title.
LD1741.E762K45 2004
378.756'58—dc22   2004000141

A catalog record for this book is available from the British Library.

ISBN 13: 978-1-4214-1497-3 (hardcover : alk. paper)
ISBN 10: 1-4214-1479-X (hardcover : alk. paper)
ISBN 13: 978-1-4214-1447-8 (pbk. : alk. paper)
ISBN 10: 1-4214-1447-3 (pbk. : alk. paper)
ISBN 13: 978-1-4214-1448-5 (electronic)
ISBN 10: 1-4214-1448-1 (electronic)

*Special discounts are available for bulk purchases of this book.
For more information, please contact
Special Sales at 410-516-6936 or specialsales@press.jhu.edu.*

Johns Hopkins University Press uses environmentally friendly book
materials, including recycled text paper that is composed of at least
30 percent post-consumer waste, whenever possible.

FOR JANE

❦ ❦ ❦

All the pleasure in life is in general ideas. But all the use of life is in specific solutions, which cannot be reached through generalities any more than a picture can be painted by knowing some rules of method. They are reached by insight, tact, and specific knowledge.

OLIVER WENDELL HOLMES JR.
Letter to Elmer Gertz
March 1, 1899

CONTENTS

Foreword, by Leo M. Lambert xi

Preface xv

ONE : Up from the Ashes 1

TWO : New Leader, New Initiatives 29

THREE : Student Life and Pleasures 41

FOUR : Elevating the Academics 57

FIVE : Financing the Rise 76

SIX : The Fruits and Ironies of Success 88

SEVEN : Analysis of an Ascent 98

Afterword, by Leo M. Lambert 109

Acknowledgments 137
Index 139

FOREWORD

When I was a finalist for the presidency of Elon in 1998, one of the most fascinating pieces I read about the institution was an article titled "The College That Transformed Itself," by George Keller, in the journal *Planning for Higher Education*. I knew about Keller's sterling reputation as author of *Academic Strategy: The Management Revolution in American Higher Education*, as a leading scholar in higher education, and as chair of the graduate program in higher education studies at the University of Pennsylvania.

Elon regularly hosts visitors from all over the globe wanting to learn more about the Elon transformation up close, and many of these visitors initially learned about the institution from George Keller's article. In 2002 I contacted George and asked him if he thought there might be interest in an expanded, updated look at Elon. His response was immediate and enthusiastic. He decried the lack of good case studies about institutions of higher education, especially ones that he described as "readable." His goal, as he described it to me, was to write a short book that college leaders could read cover to cover on a flight from New York to Chicago.

Transforming a College was an immediate success and

has been reprinted six times and translated into Japanese, Korean, and Chinese. It often sells in large quantities, as entire faculties and boards of trustees read the book as a common experience and then discuss its applicability to their own institutions. The book's themes, cautions, and questions apply to many institutions reexamining their purposes, aspirations, and strategic goals—a practice that healthy institutions engage in continually.

The questions George Keller addresses in *Transforming a College* transcend time, and hence there is still demand for the book a decade after publication. Nonetheless, readers often want to know "the rest of the story"—what has transpired at Elon since 2004? At the request of Johns Hopkins University Press, I was delighted to write an afterword to bring readers up to date on the Elon story, including our accomplishments, struggles, and ongoing questioning about our place on the national stage of American higher education.

Elon is a wonderful place, but it is not perfect, and the university is still very much a work in progress. Indeed, the excitement for all of us at Elon is the continuing work on an institution that is in the process of reaching its full potential. We have many unrealized goals, and yet the progress the university has achieved over the decades is indeed remarkable. When visitors ask me how this happened, I offer the following short list of reasons. I offer it up as a prelude to George Keller's case study.

1. Elon has kept its focus on students and their learning. As simple as this seems, other distractions can often dominate campus life.
2. Planning is a key feature of Elon's culture. Budgeting and annual objective-setting processes are linked to

ambitious, long-term strategic goals. When we set a goal or objective, everyone expects follow-through. As Thomas Edison is reported to have said, "Vision without execution is hallucination."

3. Leadership matters at every level. Elon has had only three presidents in the past fifty-six years. The senior staff of the institution has been stable and extraordinarily capable. Faculty and staff have devoted themselves to creating an engaging and enriched environment for learning—the most important kind of leadership. Trustees have set high standards of excellence.

4. Elon sets stretch goals for itself and maps out step-by-step plans to achieve them, even with modest resources.

5. Elon is constantly innovating. We visit other campuses regularly, borrow ideas, and adapt them to our own institution and culture. We avoid imitation. Institutional ossification is slow death.

6. Elon has been guided by a core set of financial principles: low tuition discount; leverage of debt to build key facilities, especially those that produce revenue; a culture of everyone working for admissions; every dollar spent needing to advance more than one goal. We have often reflected that being under-resourced encourages creativity. Of late, a shift toward building endowment has become a priority.

7. Our strong sense of institutional community and commitment to a commonly understood mission is the glue that holds everything together, especially during trying times.

8. We know who we are and what we are about—human transformation. In the end, all of the planning, bud-

geting, and hiring of personnel is not about the construction of a campus or the building of programs and
curriculum. Rather, it is about the flourishing and personal growth of each individual student, who will leave
Elon ready to assume a meaningful place in the world
and pursue a life of purpose.

I hope you will find *Transforming a College* a compelling
story. If you read it on an airplane, as George imagined,
I encourage you to think high-above-the-cloud thoughts
about your own institution, its mission and purpose,
your most audacious hopes and dreams for it, and, most
importantly, your contribution to shape the next genera-
tion of leaders our world so desperately needs.

Leo M. Lambert
President, Elon University
Elon, North Carolina

PREFACE

Higher education in the United States is unusual. Alone among the world's nations, America has without design settled on an arrangement that includes all colleges and universities in its ethos of capitalist competition. Like small and large business firms, the country's thirty-nine hundred colleges and universities are expected to scramble, strategize, and compete for students, professors, facilities, acclaim, and financial stability. If they do not, they are likely to close their doors or be closed.

This competition has pressured the 1,640 public institutions—those that receive monies from one of the fifty states—and the 2,260 private or independent colleges and universities, which rely largely on tuition and private contributions, to make themselves attractive or necessary to some segment of America's population. A polyglot nation like the United States thus has colleges or universities devoted primarily to Native Americans, African Americans, Roman Catholics, Latinos, Jews, and women. There are giant state universities—such as the University of Texas at Austin, Ohio State University, and the University of Minnesota—each of which enrolls nearly fifty thousand students a year, and there are 490 private two- and four-year colleges that each enroll fewer than five hundred students.

Americans can study jazz, rock, and contemporary popular music at Boston's Berklee College of Music; enroll in a graduate program to become a coach, athletic director, or expert in sports medicine at the U.S. Sports Academy in Daphne, Alabama; or attend an academy that trains naval officers at the U.S. Naval Academy in Annapolis, Maryland. The variety is astounding. In addition, the nation has roughly five thousand proprietary colleges, schools owned by an individual or corporation, which train persons to become airplane mechanics, medical technicians, or commercial artists, and it has a rapidly growing number of profit-making colleges and universities, such as the DeVry Institutes, the Corinthian Colleges, and the University of Phoenix.

This booming, dazzling array of institutions of higher education in the United States means that America's colleges and universities are in constant competition with each other for students, dollars, and public attention. They often buzz with talk of competitive niche, market position, product differentiation, brand, ratings, and reputation—though most dignified faculty members detest such talk. Colleges that compete poorly decline, go out of business, or merge with more secure institutions. Colleges and universities of eminence struggle to remain eminent, with frequent drives for more money, aggressive faculty recruiting, applications for research grants, more attractive architecture and the latest equipment, and shrewd, energetic solicitation of exceptional and highly talented students.

Then there are the many colleges and universities in America that neither enjoy national status nor fear closure. They are the middling many, frequently indifferent, complacent, satisfactory, and less affluent. A surprising number are trying to rise in their category from being moderately good academic institutions to becoming truly excellent and well regarded. In fact, the capitalist competition of U.S. higher education is conducive to a remarkable degree of higher aspirations and strategic efforts among the nation's academic campuses.

This little book is the story of one such college. Four decades ago Elon College in north central North Carolina was described to me by one North Carolina scholar as "a small, unattractive, parochial bottom-feeder," struggling to fill its freshman class and pay its bills. Today Elon University is a beautiful, medium-size university attracting students from forty-eight states, with a new library, student center, science facilities, football stadium, and fitness center. Parents, visitors, and students often come away from the country club–like campus with something approaching awe. College guidebooks now list it among the three hundred finest undergraduate institutions in the land.

How did this transformation occur? What can other aspiring colleges and universities learn from Elon's scrappy climb to new prominence and competitive power? And what are the fresh problems of a college that has moved from one position in the higher education firmament to another, brighter position?

What follows is an attempt to answer these questions, and others, and to identify what may be the essential ingredients of a novel kind of American collegiate education. The book is not intended to provide a recipe for increased fame or quality. Nor do I intend that other colleges emulate what Elon has done. My hope is that those at other colleges and universities can draw some inspiration and guidance from Elon's ascent. America has never needed as many highly educated, creative, spirited persons as it does today.

TRANSFORMING A COLLEGE

Up from the Ashes

🐝 🐝 🐝

W HEN DR. JULIANNE MAHER, the newly selected
vice president for academic affairs, arrived at North
Carolina's Elon College in the fall of 1995, she inquired
about the rivalries and policy disagreements on campus
to prepare herself for her first year. To her astonishment,
she was told repeatedly that there were none. In fact, she
says her repeated inquiries resulted in a few persons
wondering whether the new vice president might be
paranoid.

A year later, she still marveled about her first months.

> There are almost no petty feuds or intrigues here. Most
> faculty care for the students and teach imaginatively;
> they support each other and actually like the adminis-
> tration. And the faculty have renovated their own gen-
> eral education program. The administrators, too, are a
> talented, collaborating team. There is a very, very strong
> sense of community here at Elon.

Elon's faculty-elected Academic Council is unusually polite and constructive. There are no unions either.

The harmony at Elon is not the only unusual thing about this institution. The 575-acre campus is strikingly beautiful and pristine. There is no litter, no graffiti, and no unpruned, dead branches or unpainted white columns. Elon has no deferred maintenance—none. The institution has had more than three decades of surplus in the annual budget, and the last two capital funds campaigns, for $18 million and $40 million, finished over the top.

The college, with forty-four hundred students, has a faculty-designed general education program that goes beyond the usual Chinese-menu selections of most liberal arts colleges. There is a complementary cocurricular program called the Elon Experiences, which engages students in five areas: leadership, international studies and experiences, community service, undergraduate research, and internships and cooperative work apprenticeships. The Elon Experiences are noted on a separate transcript, which records each student's participation in out-of-class activities for potential employers and graduate schools. The annual survey of senior students regularly rates the quality of teaching as the best feature of the college, recently renamed Elon University. (Maintenance and campus beauty are second.) The seniors also rated the quality of food in the 1990s as one of the worst features, so the three old dining halls have been renovated, with the newly popular *marché* concept for wider food selection and a new set of cooks. Though hardly haute cuisine, Elon's fare is now a notch above the usual college victuals.

Since 1988 Elon has erected an astonishing twenty-seven new buildings and renovated a dozen others. Koury Center resembles the athletic facilities at some larger state universities, with a fitness center worthy of a posh resort, and the center is run in considerable part by the students themselves. The Moseley Center, a handsome $8 million student activities building, was opened in 1995, followed by six new fraternity and sorority houses in the on-campus Greek courtyard. The state-of-the-art, $18 million McMichael Science Center opened in 1998, and the stunning new Belk Library, costing $13 million, opened its doors in 2000. There is even a new $12 million, 8,250-seat football stadium and a new Olympic-quality running track. All of this has been done by a relatively poor college. Elon's endowment as of June 30, 2002, was $55.6 million, up from a meager $27 million in 1996 and $3 million in 1980. By comparison, Georgia's Berry College in 2002 had $194 million in funds, South Carolina's Furman University had $248 million, North Carolina's Davidson College possessed $318 million, Virginia's Washington & Lee owned a $438 million endowment, and the University of Richmond had $998 million.

Word of Elon University's extraordinary rise has begun to attract national attention. The dubious 2003 *U.S. News & World Report* survey ranked Elon eighth among southern universities, up from thirty-ninth in 1995, and the *Princeton Review* just added Elon to its annual book on *The Best 345 Colleges*. Parents and their sons and daughters from all over the East have begun flocking to Elon. Since 1994 the number of applications to enroll in the school has increased by 45 percent, and there has been a 119-point rise in average freshman SAT scores. Elon's students now come from forty-eight states and forty foreign countries. For the fall of 2003, Elon had more than seven thousand applications for the freshman class of twelve hundred, with the highest SAT scores ever.

The "Good" Old Days

It was not always so. When Leon Edgar Smith, '10, a pastor in the Christian Church—the small egalitarian sect that founded Elon College in 1889—became president in 1931, the college was still recovering from a disastrous 1923 fire. Enrollment had declined to only eighty-seven students, and the faculty members had received almost no pay for a year. Smith quickly mailed five hundred letters to the citizens of Alamance County asking for three dollars each to keep the college open. He received two replies for a total of thirteen dollars. He also appealed to churches and alumni and got three thousand dollars, enough to open the college again in the fall of 1932. President Smith spent most of the 1930s eluding creditors, borrowing money, and recruiting students.

By 1939 Elon College had 660 students. But when World War II began, enrollment plummeted again. The plucky Dr. Smith convinced the U.S. Army to train pilots at Elon, canceled athletics, and by what he called "almost criminal economy" managed to get the college through the war years. Then the G.I. Bill brought new students, enabling L. E. Smith, as he was known, to build a few buildings and put the college on a sound financial basis. When he retired in 1957, in his seventies, Smith had raised enrollment to 1,630 students, mainly local young women and men, and had boosted the endowment to $680,000.

His successor was a gifted young chemist on the faculty, James Earl Danieley, '46, who was only thirty-two years old. President Danieley made the College Board's Scholastic Aptitude Tests (SATs) a requirement for admission, expanded the library, built seven new buildings, registered Elon's first black students, strengthened the athletic teams, instituted a 4-1-4 semester system, encouraged all faculty to work toward their Ph.D.s, created an Academic Council, and in 1972 completed a $3 million fund drive, with strong help from the trustees.

President Danieley made Elon academically respectable, and he did so with financial acumen. Elon was one of the only colleges in the state that operated in the black repeatedly. But Danieley was also a teetotaler and an autocrat. He was exceedingly firm when unruly students and a few faculty began protesting, halting classes, and going countercultural in the late 1960s and early 1970s. Dr. Danieley's fierce commitment to keeping Elon College a special kind of small, unified academic community of increasing status was unwavering. Jo Watts Williams, the retired vice president for development, says,

> He ran a very tight ship. But he set the tone for today's college: a close, collaborative community, strong financial management, increasing academic rigor, and entrepreneurial growth.

Plagued by back problems, Danieley asked to be allowed to return to the classroom in 1973. The endowment had grown to $3 million, but indebtedness had also grown, to $3.4 million. Enrollment stood at 1,800 students, only 170 students more than when he had taken office sixteen years earlier, and many undergraduates were still local and underprepared for serious college work.

Rethinking the College

When President Danieley resigned in 1973, Elon College was scarcely known outside central North Carolina. Its dozen buildings beside the town's railroad tracks struck visitors as undistinguished, with a parking lot smack in the center of the campus. The students mostly came from working-class families in the nearby mill town of Burlington, local farming families, and religious families from nearby small towns. The academic program was solid but without distinction.

How did Elon College become one of the more attractive, up-and-coming colleges in the nation over little more than three decades? What propelled the college's officers, faculty, and trustees to reach for an ambitious new level of excellence? What were the levers, the strategies of radical change?

There were several. Perhaps the most significant was the college's surprising choice for president in the spring of 1973, J. Fred Young. He was a Baptist, a school administrator with a doctorate from Columbia Teachers College in New York. Young had been an assistant superintendent of schools in Burlington and a deputy superintendent of schools for the commonwealth of Virginia. He was only thirty-eight years old, but he was well known as an energetic and excellent administrator, and he was a North Carolinian.

President Young quickly determined that Elon College's financial situation was vulnerable, with a tiny endowment and 90 percent of the revenues coming from student tuition. Enrollment was therefore critical. His analysis of Elon's students showed that more that 90 percent came from North Carolina and Virginia and that they were overwhelmingly students of average and below-average ability from families of modest means. Young also noticed three other conditions. The state of North Carolina had opened fifty new community colleges between 1957 and 1971, including one in Alamance County, Elon's home county, and their tuition was one-fifth that of Elon's. From his experience in school administration, he knew that the baby boom had crested in 1961 and birth rates were declining; by 1979 the number of potential college students would begin to drop. And Elon College was only an hour's drive from both the famous low-cost University of North Carolina at Chapel Hill and the rapidly growing University of North Carolina at Greensboro. Moreover, a good Quaker school, Guilford College, was close by, and another institution of the United Church of Christ (into which the Congregational Christian Church had merged), Catawba College, was only sixty miles to the southwest.

"We thought we would lose students by the 1980s, so we had to scramble," Young says. The new president made admissions and the improvement of student life programs his first priorities. He redesigned the admissions materials, rearranged his administrative structure, initiated new majors, opened a campus radio station, and brought in student honor societies. James Moncure, Young's vice president for student and academic affairs, reflected the president's views in a 1974 article for the *Elon Magazine:*

> The place of a small liberal arts school in the future rests in the quality of student life. The mammoth universities will have facilities as good as those in the small colleges, but the behemoth institutions cannot provide the

life style, the maturing environment . . . Elon College knows this and is doing something about it.

President Young felt that a major handicap to attracting more students was the appearance of the campus. Elon had grown with little regard for Frederick Law Olmsted's nineteenth-century admonition that a well-designed campus was integral to the higher education of students, improving the "tastes, inclinations, and habits" of the young. Fred Young therefore did two things. When in 1974 two trustees urged him to buy a forty-three-acre property north of Haggard Avenue so that the college could one day build a beautiful north campus opposite the old south campus, he quickly agreed. And in 1975 he contracted with Lewis Clarke Associates to devise a master plan for landscaping, beautification, and growth. These were, historically, an important pair of decisions.

The architectural firm assigned a young, talented, self-assured landscape architect, A. Wayne McBride Jr., to lead the creation of Elon College's master plan. His previous experience was mainly in designing resorts for the affluent. When Young told McBride that he wanted to make the Elon campus more attractive to parents and their offspring, McBride immediately understood. He remembers feeling "that a college campus and a resort are quite similar. Both need to be lovely places at which you want to stay and visit often. Most parents want to feel that a college is safe, clean, and beautiful, with creature comforts alongside first-rate teaching."

McBride found Elon's architecture to be plain and the landscaping awful. There were almost no cordial open spaces. A parking lot stood smack in the middle of the main quadrangle formed by the Powell, Duke, Alamance, and Carlton buildings. "I decided to go all-out and design a strikingly handsome place, a storybook southern college." He proposed new athletic fields, a large field house, and development of the small lake on the college's grounds. Where the parking lot stood, McBride proposed a large, dramatic fountain.

When the faculty saw the drawings, they were thunderstruck and hung a huge sign that read "Welcome to Disneyland." Two of the trustees were also against such a bold and radical renovation and expansion of the campus. According to McBride,

> Fred Young, too, was a bit nervous, even though he deeply believed in the importance of a more attractive setting. He used to call me every week or two to get assurances that my plan would work.

But in 1976 the trustees approved the daring master plan and initiated a $5.5 million fund drive to make it a reality.

Looking back, Fred Young remembers that "in those days fear was our great motivator." Elon was tuition-dependent, so the college had to concentrate on enrollment. To get more and better students, Elon needed a lovelier campus, new residence halls, a richer student life, and improved academic programs.

To tackle the academic side, the college's leaders applied for a $2 million grant from the federal government's Advanced Institutional Development Program (AIDP) in Title III of the Higher Education Act, and in June 1977 the college was notified that it had received the grant, to be used over five years. According to Young, "This grant was what enabled us to take off." The money was to be used to elevate Elon College to a new level of instruction and service, and college leaders, with widespread faculty help, did just that.

The curriculum was revised; a Learning Resource Center was established for remedial work and tutoring; the most talented students were groomed for professional schools and graduate school fellowships; an enlarged career planning and placement office was established; student counseling was improved, as were residential life programs; and institutional research, evaluations, and planning were greatly enhanced. The Title III grant had a profound effect. As a bonus, Elon's football team, the Fighting Christians, went to the National Association of Intercollegiate Athletics (NAIA) finals in 1978 and then won the national championship in 1980 and 1981.

The flurry of new initiatives led to increased support. More alumni, friends, and trustees began to contribute to Elon. In 1979 the federal government provided a low-interest, $2.8 million loan to build new dormitories for the students, and the Z. Smith Reynolds Foundation approved a grant of $350,000 to establish a new fund-raising program for deferred and planned gifts.

Repositioning the College

By 1979, enrollment had grown to twenty-five hundred students, a 38 percent increase since 1973. Through exceedingly frugal management, the college ran a modest surplus every year, using the extra dollars to improve facilities and purchase equipment. The combination of conservative budgeting and the double financial injections from additional students and from small tuition increases provided these annual surpluses. This meant that Elon College had the equivalent of some venture capital for growth each year. But growth toward what?

In 1976 Elon College changed its charter from being "under the general control" of the United Church of Christ to being "affiliated with" the church, and the percentage of trustees who had to belong to the United Church of Christ was reduced to one-sixth. This change, plus the increased number of students, the campus master plan, the college's first large foundation grant—$1 million from the Spencer Love Foundation—and growing faculty pride encouraged President Young to think more comprehensively about the future.

Fred Young never stopped worrying about demographics, enrollment, and marketing. According to one of his former close aides: "Fred was an absolute nut about the importance of admissions, retention, and marketing. He never let anyone forget that." The main admissions office is still next to the president's office. But Elon's momentum, the college's approaching centennial in 1989, and trustee pressure for improved academic quality prompted a more thoughtful look ahead, a strategic design toward some new distinction.

Young therefore formed a marketing task force in the early 1980s. The group studied Elon's constituency and the competition and surveyed the students. "We found that the students really liked us—the great teaching, the friendly community, the new attention to facilities and more attractive grounds," declares Nan Perkins, an ex-English instructor and then the director of communications.

The task force findings gradually were fused with the leadership's awareness that Elon was located in a state with an ideally moderate climate and between the Research Triangle, Duke University, and the flagship University of North Carolina (UNC) at Chapel Hill to the east and UNC-Greensboro in a rapidly growing city twenty miles west. Both Raleigh-Durham and Greensboro had good airports, and a major highway, Interstate 40-85, ran between them. Alan White, professor of physical education and director of athletics, has been at Elon since 1974. His assessment is that "Elon College has a marvelous location in a nice, small town between two expanding urban areas, which both have several other colleges and universities."

These new awarenesses resulted in what Young now describes as a "major repositioning" of Elon College. The college leaders decided, with pressure from the trustees, to create a different kind of college for a different clientele. Instead of admitting relatively weak students of modest means (with combined SATs of 750 to 1000) mainly from North Carolina and southern Virginia, Elon College would strive to admit more middle-class and even some wealthy students with average and above-average SATs (900 to 1300) from the entire eastern half of the nation and abroad. "We went after the students who couldn't get into Davidson, Duke, or Princeton," says one administrator. (In the 1982 *Kudzu-Ivy Guide to Southern Colleges*, Elon was still described as a "nice small school that takes C students and seems to care about helping them.")

The board of trustees was highly influential in this repositioning. They pressed the president to move Elon from being a low-cost to a medium-cost college and to raise entrance requirements. "I would not have had the nerve to do that without the trustees pushing me," Young says.

Elon trustees and officials seemed to recognize two things. First, there were many thousands of delightful, genial young women and men who were not in the top tenth of their graduating high school classes and who had combined SAT scores slightly above the national average of 920 (or 1010 in the College Board's "recentered" SAT scores). Second, they noticed that the Ivy League universities, Duke, Stanford, and the dozen or so finest and most highly endowed elite liberal arts colleges were increasingly turning away from readily accepting the children of wealthy families and alumni and prep school graduates and were admitting mainly the very brightest young scholars from many social, racial, and economic backgrounds.

This, Elon's leaders decided, could be their niche: students from loving, affluent families with average and slightly above-average academic credentials. Realistically, Elon had little choice. While Davidson College had $92,000 of endowment behind each student and Guilford had $27,200, Elon College had only $6,800 of endowment per student. Elon could not afford to hand out many scholarships and grants, and college leaders felt strongly that Elon had to keep its tuition as low as possible for competitive reasons.

The Remaking of Elon

Once Elon College decided on its new student market, the priority of initiatives became clearer. The admissions office started recruiting in "bleeder" states—where a relatively high percentage of high school students go out of state for college or university—like Maryland, Delaware, New Jersey, Pennsylvania, Ohio, New York, and Connecticut, as well as in Georgia and Florida. The admissions staff began calling at prep schools. Nearly 22 percent of Elon's students now come from private high schools, and only 30 percent of Elon's students are from North Carolina.

To attract a more affluent and geographically diverse student clientele, Elon's leaders had to make the campus and its buildings more modern and attractive. So the executives and trustees raised money aggressively and borrowed heavily to finance a flurry of new buildings and facility renovations. The Duke Science Building was renovated, as were the main dining halls, the computer labs, and the historic Alamance Building. At the urging of one trustee especially, a modern but not very well-designed fine arts building opened in 1987. New residence halls went up, as did the Koury Center, six new Greek houses, and the Jimmy Powell Tennis Center, which *Tennis Industry* magazine proclaimed in 1989 as one of the ten finest new tennis facilities in the nation. (Elon has a long history of strong tennis teams.)

The Fonville Fountain replaced the parking lot, which made a big difference. Fred Young claims that "the fountain changed our sense of self and how visiting parents and others see us." The president became fanatical about the cleanliness and beauty of the campus. He gave talks about civility and respect and urged faculty, staff, and students to pick up litter, as he himself always did, and to report anything that was broken so it could be fixed immediately.

More importantly, the academic programs were rearranged. The two-year A.A. degrees in secretarial science and medical lab technician studies were abolished, and the college stopped admitting marginal students. The business program was strengthened, and new majors in communications, computer systems, and leisure/sports management were introduced. Two master's degree programs—an M.B.A. in business and an M.Ed. in education—were started.

To teach the new clientele of students, Elon College hired—carefully selected may be more appropriate—numerous young professors, more than any other private college in North Carolina during the 1980s. The hiring was done by the departments but supervised and directed by Warren Board, then Elon's provost and after 1994 the president of Saint Andrews College in North Carolina, and by Gerald Francis, a mathematics professor who is the current provost. Michael Sanford, a member of the visual arts department, recalls that "Warren Board was a great visionary. Gerry Francis was cautious and vigilant. They were a terrific pair. Those two transformed the faculty." According to Michael Calhoun, a young associate professor of health education and leisure/sports management, "We have a small faculty group that still calls itself 'the Class of 1985' because we think some remarkable hotshots were hired that year." The number of faculty at Elon College in the 1980s went from 74 to 125.

Several of the new faculty pressed Elon's provost and deans to institute "Writing across the Curriculum" and to provide opportunities for them to learn to teach better, with more critical thinking and the use of computers. Clair Myers, dean of arts and humanities at that time, credits Barbara Gordon, associate professor of English and now director of the Writing Program, with stimulating efforts in the mid-1980s. The faculty were given some money, and Elon professors brought in outside speakers and experts, attended "critical thinking" workshops at the University of Chicago, went on retreats, and organized teaching workshops. They learned to collaborate and help each other. Michael Calhoun sees "almost no departmental isolation here. It's quite unusual." Calhoun, an expert in sport science, teaches a freshman seminar in global studies. Many professors reduced their lecturing and introduced more active learning and Socratic questioning into their classes.

Elon College's repositioning was expensive, particularly the new buildings and additional faculty. How could the college afford its liftoff? To finance change, college leaders used an ingenious array of methods.

The college continued to run surpluses. It raised the percentage of alumni giving from about 15 percent in the early 1970s to nearly 30 percent by 1990. The board of trustees was "transformed," says Jo Watts Williams, and the loyal friends, prominent executives, and community leaders on the board of trustees gave increasingly generous support. Annual private support jumped from $950,000 in 1979 to $2.8 million by 1989. The college also borrowed boldly—some said alarmingly—raising its debt to roughly $12 million. And Elon was fortunate to be able to draw on very capable part-time faculty who lived in the Greensboro to Chapel Hill and Durham corridor.

Creating Distinctiveness

"A fine-quality institution is never static," President Young told the faculty and staff repeatedly. As the 1990s began he and his cabinet formulated a "Plan for the 90s." It was both limited and radical, and it had three aims: a new, forward-looking, and distinctive academic and cocurricular program; additional facilities and campus landscaping for the more affluent students that the college was beginning to attract; and increased academic quality. Young began to talk about making Elon College "one of the best institutions of its kind on the eastern seaboard." He was convinced that two things were necessary to accomplish this jump in stature: a distinctive academic and extracurricular program and exceptional quality in everything that Elon did—from the physical appearance of the campus and the college's financial management to classroom teaching and career planning for the students. The trustees voted to begin an $18 million capital campaign to finance the push toward regional distinction, and the trustees themselves pledged $5 million.

In 1991 the faculty and deans began meeting to devise a distinctive, future-oriented curriculum, under the leadership of Gerald Francis. The usual course throughout academe is for such faculty meetings to go on for years, often producing pygmy, politicized alterations. At first, Elon's faculty behaved similarly. The chairperson of the general education overhaul, Russell Gill (a talented professor of English with a Harvard Ph.D.), was a devotee of the widest possible democratic participation. The discussions dragged on. An expert mediator from Washington, D.C., was brought in. "She was great," one dean says. But the provost and deans finally had to force some decisions.

It was Provost Francis who broke through the shilly-shallying. He offered what amounted to a radical change in the nature of academic work at Elon by suggesting that most classes meet for four hours each week, instead of the traditional three hours, and carry four hours of credit. The additional hours, he proposed, should be used to incorporate active learning techniques into the classes. Nearly 150 courses in the catalog would be cut, and the faculty's teaching load would be reduced from nine courses a year to six.

Many of Elon's teachers were skeptical of the proposal

because it would require a major reconstruction of each academic department's array of offerings, would alter many professors' preferred mode of instruction (lecturing), and would reduce the breadth of course offerings for students. According to Francis, it was Lela Faye Rich, with her research on Elon's students and her arguments, who "broke the logjam."

Lela Faye Rich, at that time an assistant professor of history and the director of advising and career services and now associate dean for academic support services, is an imaginative, lively, outspoken person. As one faculty member describes her, "Lela Faye is never shy about expressing her ideas and feelings, and she has been a powerful influence on our thinking about how best to teach Elon's students." Dozens of consultants have counseled colleges to study their students, to know more thoroughly what kind of students are coming through their doors. Few colleges, however, do so. But at Elon, Rich gives each entering student a Myers-Briggs Type Indicator test and studies each student with uncommon diligence. She believes deeply that "a college's curriculum, teaching styles, extracurricular life, and counseling must match the profile of its students."

What Rich has found is that the Myers-Briggs test reveals year after year that Elon College attracts mainly a specific type of student. (The test divides all persons into sixteen types, defining each type by such attributes as introvert or extrovert, sensing or intuitive, thinking or feeling, and perceptive or judging.) "Elon is full of student extroverts who are big on sensing, feeling, and doing things rather than sitting alone in libraries," says Rich.

Our primary type is ENFP, or extroverted intuition with feeling, and the second most prominent is ESTJ, or extroverted thinking with sensing. I love it, because I'm an ENFP myself.

Rich claims that ENFPs are less likely to excel on standardized tests and tend to love their friends, travel, internships, real-life experiences, and extracurricular activities as much as they like working with books or in laboratories. But many of Elon's professors, like those at other universities, are INTJs (introverted with thinking) and INTPs (introverted thinking with intuition). They tend to be bookish, more interested in theory than participation in real-life experiences, and inclined to thought rather than action. Thus, Elon had a mismatch between its scholarly, pensive faculty and its mostly ebullient body of students.

So, at this critical juncture in the institution's growth, Rich forcefully lobbied for a new curriculum and array of studies—a novel general education program—that is highly experiential to fit the kind of undergraduates that Elon had in its midst. The trick, she suggested, was to design an academic program that somehow combined the faculty's preferred way of teaching with the students' preferred way of learning. As she put it, "You can't design a curriculum for nerds when the students are not nerds." That is what she argued in the general education discussions. Finally, 60 percent of the faculty voted to support Provost Francis's proposed changes.

The general education program that emerged in 1993–94 was highly experiential, with students required to take a first-year seminar in the "global experience" and encouraged to study abroad in such programs as Art in Italy, Astronomy in Mexico, or Economics in Europe; required

to take two courses in "expression," such as dance, literature, theater or fine arts, or philosophy; and encouraged
to engage in internships in business, government, or
social services. All students also had to take a wellness
course, which Michael Calhoun describes this way:

> We ask them to examine themselves and their lifestyles
> physically, socially, sexually, and spiritually. We force
> them to explore what they must do to live a long, healthy,
> active, and possibly important life.

To undergird the active proclivities of Elon's students,
the college added an impressive fitness facility to the
Koury Center and constructed a large, handsome student
center, Moseley Center, on the north campus, close to the
student residence halls. Also, Elon assembled an unusual
cocurricular program and kept the sports program so
strong that for most years Elon College has won the South
Athletic Conference Excellence Award for the best overall athletics program. To Provost Francis, "1992 to 1994
were our watershed years."

As Elon repositioned itself as a different kind of college for a different and more diverse clientele, President
Young worried about the possible defection of some of
the loyal, older graduates and the snipping of the college's Christian roots. He was concerned that character,
service, and values formation somehow remain part of
an Elon education. So, alongside the renovation of the
academic program, the college created what the president called the Elon Experiences. These cocurricular experiences were initially composed of four separate but coordinated experiences. One was study abroad, a particular
favorite of the president, who felt that preparation for
intercultural and international life is essential. A second

was volunteer service, encouraging students to help those less fortunate. For instance, Elon was the first college in America that committed to erecting or renovating a house each year for the Habitat for Humanity program. The school donates $5,000, but the students must raise the other $25,000 to build each house for the poor.

A third part of the Elon Experiences was the increasingly popular work in outside firms as interns or co-op students; nearly 80 percent of the students now have work experience. And the fourth piece was leadership development, launched with the demanding Isabella Cannon Leadership Program, which added dozens of leadership opportunities on campus. According to Smith Jackson, vice president of student life:

> Elon has the most active students I've ever seen. They run their own conferences. They did 58,000 hours of community service last year. They helped open a new coffeehouse on Williamson Avenue. They are highly self-confident doers. What many lack, though, is self-confidence in their intellectual skills. But that is changing. Our faculty are marvelous in mentoring them toward academic strength.

Jackson also devised a separate cocurricular transcript so that graduating students can show their potential employers all the activities, experiences, jobs, and leadership positions in which they were involved as undergraduates at Elon.

President Young became proud of the Elon Experiences, each of which has its own office. "We chose four values—work, service, leadership, and cultural understanding—and made them the modern college's equivalent of old-time religious inculcation."

Quality Everywhere

The new academic and cocurricular program gave Elon College a distinctive, competitive approach to educating the whole student—in mind, body, service, leadership skills, work, and spirit. The other prong of Young's efforts in the early 1990s was his passion for instilling quality everywhere, from registration procedures to the pageantry of the graduation ceremony. Two operations that responded especially well were the business office and facilities maintenance.

In 1992 the college lured a young financial executive away from Agnes Scott College in Georgia, at the time the fifth-richest college per student in the country, with an endowment of $252 million for 570 women students. Gerald Whittington decided to come to penurious Elon College, as its vice president for business and finance, "because of the challenge and where it was going." Whittington, an outwardly calm but creative and audacious financial executive, was a brilliant choice for the ambitious but underfinanced school. As he says,

> During the 1990s we reengineered the whole college. We've outsourced. We've done TQM. We've benchmarked. We've done strategic planning. Only we never called our initiatives by those labels.

Whittington quickly modernized the computer system for the administration and for better financial control. He looked at Elon's endowment and found it heavily invested in bonds and cash, appreciating and earning very little. So he and the trustees' investment committee divided the endowment among one bond house and three investment houses specializing in stocks: one in value stocks, one in growth stocks, and a contrarian outfit. When the stock market jumped forward in the late 1990s, the value of Elon's small endowment rose nearly 40 percent.

With the help of a consultant, Whittington created the college's own medical insurance plan to reduce the cost of medical fringe benefits. The plan was changed from an old-style indemnity plan to a stop-loss plan, where the college pays 70 percent and the employees pay 30 percent. It set up a network of physicians and hospitals who agreed to reduce their fees in return for Elon's employees using their services. The benefits are capped but at a reasonably high level. A wellness education campaign was launched among the faculty and staff to counsel them about risky behaviors, and programs in smoking cessation, nutrition, and blood pressure and diabetes screening were introduced.

Vice President Whittington, President Young, and Provost Francis set a policy for the financial aid office to hold grants from tuition revenues for new students to a mere 12 percent. (Many colleges are now spending a financially dangerous 35–40 percent of their tuition revenues for financial aid grants to attract new students.) In 1993 Whittington did a comparative study of the number of administrators per faculty member and per student and found that Elon College had the lowest staffing ratio of any similar institution. He advised that the college continue to stay administratively lean and work harder and smarter than the others. Elon has done so.

When Whittington discovered that many students disliked the food, he researched the latest trends in institutional food service and took a team of students, staff, and faculty on the road to visit the best college eateries. During 1996 the college's dining halls were redesigned, and the food choices and preparation changed.

Whittington and Gerald Francis also gave budget outlook presentations to the faculty and staff each year to help every office prepare its next year's budget wisely, as several other financially astute universities now do. The pudgy and witty vice president for business and finance asserts with pride, "Elon is the little engine that could."

Beginning in 1995 the maintenance and care of Elon's grounds and facilities came into the hands of a lean, sprightly, waggish former commander in the U.S. Navy's Civil Engineering Corps, Neil Bromilow. While in the navy he had helped to build a NATO air station and naval base in Iceland. (He has recently been made director of construction on the campus because of all the new buildings going up.) When I first visited his office in 1995, the entranceway had a large hand-made poster created by some students: "Physical Plant. We really appreciate your hard work and dedication. Your residence life friends in South Area." How many buildings and grounds crews in higher education receive such love-and-gratitude posters from the undergraduates? Year after year the students claim that the appearance of the campus is one of the best things about living at Elon.

Elon's ten-person grounds crew—"the morning patrol"—is out every morning at seven making sure that the entire campus is spick and span. They clean every bathroom by eight. "We still treat our operation like show business. For us, a new show begins every day at Elon at 8:00 a.m.," Bromilow says. The staff cleans and paints nearly every dormitory room each year, and the maintenance staff rushes to make repairs. Until recently the crew planted one hundred new trees a year, mostly white oaks. (*Elon* is the Hebrew word for oak tree.) The groundskeepers have divided the campus into four zones for gardening, and each crew tries to outdo the others in beauty. Architect McBride, who still presides over the appearance of the grounds, restricts the new plants to those that are indigenous to the mid-South. In spring the campus is ablaze with colorful flowers.

By the late 1990s dozens of parents were writing letters to President Young and other campus executives praising the horticulture, cleanliness, and beauty of the campus. Visiting parents gape, take photos, and marvel. Even McBride is now impressed. "There's been a real transformation into one of the South's loveliest campuses."

A major contributor to Elon's leap into excellence has been its extensive use of outside consultants and visits by college leaders to study the best practices elsewhere. Gerry Gaff, an expert on college general education programs, helped with the curriculum reform. Vincent Tinto, the noted retention scholar at Syracuse University, advised on the importance of freshman-year bonding among students. Professors from Harvard have conducted workshops at Elon on the use of case studies. Keith Moore, an authority on college relations with the public and media, has helped with the communications of the college. And several others have lectured, advised, and assisted. One of President Young's close aides said in 1996: "Fred is a terrific listener. He's no Clark Kerr, but he sifts shrewdly through advice and learns amazingly fast." Another added that

Fred keeps changing himself, keeps growing and enlarging his vision, keeps learning and trying. He's probably an ENFP, an extroverted intuition with feeling, like the students!

The university also sends out study squads. Elon staff, faculty, and students studied America's outstanding college fitness centers and student centers before building their own. Provost Francis remembers that, "for the new library we were planning, I and five others visited ten of the best college libraries to learn the finest features to put into our new library." Whittington boasts that

> our Belk Library has every bell, whistle, and digital whatnot. I suspect it is one of the best college libraries in the country. To design it, we hired the firm of Shepley, Bulfinch, Richardson and Abbott in Boston, possibly the finest library architects in the country.

But Where's the Vision?

In late August 1994, President Young went before the faculty and staff in McCrary Theatre to proclaim, "We have completed the plan for the 1990s in just four years." He also announced that Elon had surpassed the $18 million fund-raising goal one year ahead of schedule and that the new general studies program was about to begin that fall of 1994. Not typical of him, he almost exulted: "We stand at the pinnacle after several decades of unprecedented growth. Our accomplishments surround us."

But a year earlier, Chairman of the Board of Trustees Wallace Chandler had asked the president, "What kind of institution do you want Elon to be?" So a task force composed of trustees, faculty, and staff was assembled to concoct what came to be known as the Elon Vision. The vision stated that the college will no longer try to grow much bigger; it will stay under four thousand undergraduates so it can remain a relatively tight-knit, harmonious community.

The vision had four other components. One was an overdue increase in faculty salaries. (The faculty received a sizable boost in pay in 1997–98.) Another component was an increase in academic quality through still-stronger students and some new professors. The 1996 senior student survey revealed that Elon still had some weak professors, and a few departments had not yet developed appealing, active learning approaches and internships. Some faculty complained that the students should be better prepared and more eager to learn, though Vice President for Student Life Smith Jackson contended that "we have a great niche. We shouldn't lust for a college full of highly intellectual students nor for research-oriented professors who don't care about educating young people."

The third component of the strategic plan consisted of three new facilities: a state-of-the-art library, a new science building, and an 8,250-seat stadium—about $45 million worth of architectural design and construction. And the fourth piece was a doubling of the endowment to $50 million. This fourth target was thought to be the hardest for President Young. As one of his associates said, "Fred was a fabulous admissions president and college builder. But he's not been an endowment president. Suddenly he had to grow in a new direction." Whittington agrees: "The college had to borrow money and sacrifice endowment growth to reengineer itself and build a new first-rate campus. Fund-raising had become central." But Young was undaunted. "Look, I've been president of *four* different Elons," he said with a laugh. He meant the Elon College he inherited, the college that grew from 1979 to 1989, the Elon that was transformed from 1990 to 1995, and the institution soon after. Young announced that Elon would launch a $40 million capital funds campaign to implement the Elon Vision and make it a reality.

By 1997 Elon had become a distinctively different institution and one that had actually grown more cohesive as an academic community. On Tuesday mornings many from the entire campus take a thirty-minute break to gather around the once-controversial fountain to drink coffee or soft drinks and eat doughnuts, bagels with cream cheese, or fruit. At this break, students can talk with several professors, the president, some maintenance staff, or a trustee who occasionally shows up. Chaplain Richard McBride might be preparing to honor some Hometown Heroes in a program he invented. Elon University may have reengineered itself in recent years, but it somehow has remained the surprising, cordial community that Julianne Maher found on her arrival in the fall of 1995.

But in 1997 the college had to contend with a surprising announcement by President Young.

New Leader, New Initiatives

🐛 🐛 🐛

IN THE FALL OF 1997, Elon College seemed to be rolling toward new distinction. Applications for admission had increased again, by a remarkable 15 percent. The 1995 strategic plan, the Elon Vision, was being implemented. Faculty salaries had been raised, and fresh young scholars were being recruited, screened, and hired. The new curriculum was in place. A new science building was being built, aided by a large gift from the grateful grandparent and parents of an Elon student, and an innovative $13 million library was being designed. President Young was busy raising money for both of these structures and for the football stadium he wanted very much to construct. He had collected pledges and checks for more than $30 million of the $40 million capital funds campaign then in progress. And the stock market was still increasing its multiples.

Then, on November 11, 1997, Young celebrated his birthday. He was sixty-four and had been president at Elon since 1973, for twenty-four years. He seemed as energetic as ever. But he decided that fall that it was time for him to retire, so after the Christmas holiday he notified the trustees, faculty, and staff that he would leave on December 31, 1998. The people of Elon were dazed. Young had been their leader for so long. He was the person who had pulled, planned, managed, and persistently nudged Elon away from insufficiency and mediocrity toward something greater and brighter.

According to Young, "The time was right." The pieces of the Elon Vision were falling into place, and a new strategic plan would soon be needed for the next stage of Elon's growth. The $40 million campaign was nearing completion. And Young felt that the college had reached a point in its history where it needed new and slightly different leadership.

There were other contributing factors. For one, Young loved being a hands-on manager, but as Elon College had grown he had became more and more removed from the many details he loved to oversee and make perfect. Two other reasons, as he confessed in an interview with the editor of the Council of Independent Colleges' newsletter the *Independent* (Summer 1998), were his beliefs that he was not a skillful fund-raiser nor a leader for the academic component of the college. With typical candor, he said: "I don't think advancement has been one of my real strengths. I think institutional positioning has been my strength."

Young also felt that he was fundamentally a school administrator who had grown into an effective college administrator and a results-oriented planner. He told the interviewer, "I'm a planner. It's so darn hard for me to not say where and what I am going to be doing." But he recognized, too, that he was not an intellectual or scholar, and Elon now needed a more scholarly leader to lift it to national academic renown. Wistfully, he said,

> I would have loved to have been a very creative academic administrator [but] it's not something I feel I have contributed. We have a fine academic program but . . . the faculty and others created it.

The trustees moved nimbly, forming a committee to search for a new president. The committee of fourteen—nine trustees, two faculty members, two administrators, and one student—was chaired by a serene and exceptionally astute trustee, Noel Allen, '69, of Allen and Pinnix, a law firm in Raleigh, North Carolina. The committee hired a consultant to help with the selection process, advertised for the position, and began seeking candidates through many channels. In a few months the members had more than 145 applicants. Slowly, carefully, they winnowed the list to a handful that seemed especially appropriate for Elon's presidency.

The search committee recognized that Young's successor had to have the drive, strategic planning skills, readiness to innovate, and capacity for promoting harmony exhibited by President Young but be more of a scholar and fund-raiser as well as being a comfortable communicator in national associations and important academic gatherings. After interviews, the choice was narrowed to two candidates. Two search committee members then flew to the campuses of each of the two finalists and inquired widely about them.

The New Man in Town

One of the two finalists was a personable, forty-two-year-old vice chancellor for academic affairs at the University of Wisconsin–La Crosse. He had recently been named by *Change* magazine as one of the rising young leaders in U.S. higher education. Leo Michael Lambert had had a meteoric rise into the ranks of academic leadership. At the tender age of twenty-three, he had already become assistant director of the innovative Living-Learning Center at the University of Vermont. When he left to earn a Ph.D. at Syracuse University in New York State, he soon completed his degree—in higher education—and began teaching at Syracuse University's Graduate School of Education. After a few years he was selected as associate dean of the graduate school, where he also directed an externally funded program to prepare graduate students for teaching in academe, especially at the undergraduate level. After writing articles and two books on how to prepare college teachers and evaluate their performance, he was asked to become an associate vice chancellor—and a professor—at La Crosse, Wisconsin.

In July 1996 Dr. Lambert was named provost and vice chancellor at the Wisconsin school. Twenty-one months later he received a letter informing him that someone had nominated him for the presidency of a North Carolina college named Elon. He says, "Elon was not well known in the Midwest, so I put the letter aside." Then came another invitation to apply, and he sent in his credentials. At the October 1998 meeting of Elon's board of trustees, Leo Lambert was selected as the college's eighth president. Gail Drew, a trustee and vice chair of the search committee, explains:

> He struck us as an innovator, a scholar of teaching, and an immensely engaging person. When I visited his campus at La Crosse, his secretary shed tears when she

learned Dr. Lambert might be leaving. We thought he must be special.

Lambert was a member of the United Church of Christ, with which the university is still loosely affiliated. But a few trustees and faculty wondered about his ability to raise money for Elon and its lofty ambitions. That concern was overcome, however, because it was thought that both James Earl Danieley, the former president who was still teaching at Elon and who knew many graduates, and Jo Watts Williams, the former vice president for development, could serve as guides and mentors.

Lambert remembers that, when he arrived at Elon, everyone was extraordinarily warm and welcoming and that, during his first five months in early 1999, Sara Peterson, assistant to the president, arranged a transition program to introduce him to alumni, students, faculty groups, and community leaders. "She was wonderful," says Lambert, and Gail Drew reports that "Sara Peterson's arrangements and sensitivity during the search process were awesome." In fact, Lambert found nearly the entire senior staff at Elon to be "amazingly strong."

The new president made two personnel changes several months after he arrived. One was to eliminate the position of vice president for academic affairs, which was held by Julianne Maher. The position seemed to him redundant with the provost position of Gerald Francis, and it confused faculty about who was really in charge of academic and faculty matters. Dr. Maher, now executive vice president at Wheeling College in West Virginia, says the change was handled as nicely as possible. She loved Elon even though she had begun to worry that it might be "losing its soul" by becoming too large and admitting too few disadvantaged students of talent because of Elon's lack of endowment and inability to provide many scholarships.

The other personnel change was the appointment of a new vice president of development when incumbent Jack Barner decided to move to another college. According to many, the person hired turned out to be a poor choice. He stayed less than a year. Lambert then looked within and selected Nan Perkins, the sociable, very able dean of admissions and financial planning, who had radically transformed the admissions program in her eleven years as director, to assume the vice presidency for institutional advancement. She moved into the new office, in beautiful Holland House, the former home of Presidents Danieley and Young, in April 2000, confident that Susan Klopman, her lively, experienced top aide in admissions, could continue to produce great results for the college.

With the expert work of campaign director Michael Magoon, Perkins promptly helped complete the $40 million campaign, which ended in 2001 with $47.6 million in new monies. She is now planning for the next capital gifts campaign of roughly $100 million and hiring new associates for her staff. As she did in admissions, she has developed several strategic priorities. One is to increase gifts from foundations, which Elon's leaders have not pursued actively in the past. Another two priorities are to increase gifts from corporations and to multiply the number of deferred gifts and donations in the wills of the elderly. New persons have been hired to propel all three. Perkins is pleased with Elon's unusually active parents giving program, but she thinks that "we are probably ten years away from building a strong alumni base of support." Elon has awarded more baccalaureate degrees in the past eight years than the college did from its founding in 1889 to 1995. Fewer than 30 percent of all Elon graduates currently make an annual contribution to the university.

Elon has hired a new director of alumni and parent relations, Dr. Cindy Wall Sarwi, '87, who admits that the alumni program needs to be refurbished. "I plan to vitalize Elon's alumni program so that more of our graduates will be inclined to help the university in a variety of ways." It was not until the late 1990s that Elon began to pay serious attention to alumni relations.

One of the surprising consequences of President Young's major repositioning of Elon College and its aggressive, redirected admissions drive of the late 1980s and the 1990s, with its new, more affluent students, was a profound shift in the kind of parents that the college encountered. They were often more educated, more ambitious for their offspring, more inquisitive about Elon's care for undergraduates, and more willing to assist the college—at least while their sons or daughters were in attendance. Since Elon was a relatively underfinanced college, it was delighted to receive the help of the more activist parents. Elon created a Parents Council of one hundred families, twenty-five from each undergraduate class. Prospective members are identified by the admissions office and are then invited to join the council by a letter from the president.

Mary Ruth, '66, who served as director of alumni and parent relations from 1995 until her departure in December 2002, says that "the Parents Council has become so popular that we now have dozens of parents lobbying and pleading to be admitted." (She left to work at an American Indian School in Albuquerque, New Mexico.)

New Leader, New Initiatives

The council meets each October and April to hear a state-of-the-university report from President Lambert and meet in committees that advise the administration about student life issues. Ruth reported that many of the parents on the council are so curious and eager that she had to devote nearly one-third of her already busy schedule to their questions, suggestions, and concerns.

The Parents Council has raised $150,000 to endow a scholarship, named after Ruth, and they collected $250,000 recently to construct a new health center to assure that their children—and others—receive the finest health care while at the university. Almost one-third of all Elon parents now make an annual gift to the school in addition to paying tuition. Warren "Dusty" Rhodes, the father of an Elon graduate, offered a large gift to help build the $12 million football stadium that Elon had wanted on campus for the fifty-five years its football teams had to play in Burlington's municipal stadium. His $2 million gift in 1997 led college leaders to name the facility Rhodes Stadium.

Games the College Plays

The building of Rhodes Stadium between 1999 and 2001 was a typically well-researched project and presented an unpleasant surprise. Elon executives benchmarked the best college stadiums and hired the Kansas City firm of Ellerbe Becket, the nation's outstanding stadium architects, who had designed the acclaimed Camden Yards Stadium in Baltimore. The field's surface has real grass, a special variety of Bermuda grass, like that used by the National Football League. The stands for the 8,250 spectators are commodious. And the stadium's McKinnon Field, named after trustee Bob McKinnon and his wife,

Ray, was built larger than usual so that major soccer games could also be played in the stadium.

But when the contractors started excavating for the stadium, they discovered an underground lake beneath the site. Construction director Neil Bromilow says, "Fortunately the college is located on the highest point in Alamance County, so we were able to install pipes for downhill drainage." Extra sand was laid beneath the playing field so that the grass surface is relatively dry soon after a heavy rain. The stadium itself is unusually attractive, with a bell tower and brick archways. When it opened on September 22, 2001, a sellout crowd of nine thousand came to see it, some pitching tents in a grassy area called "The Green" behind the Moseley Center, thus beginning festive tailgating Saturdays like those many other colleges and universities have long enjoyed.

To nearly everyone's surprise a marching band cheekily calling itself The Fire of the Carolinas also appeared, complete with new maroon-and-white uniforms. President Leo Lambert thought a marching band for Elon might be appropriate, and a query had been sent to all undergraduates asking whether anyone would be interested. To athletic director Alan White's delight, more than eighty students asked to be in the band.

The stadium is only part of Elon's strategic initiative to become a more prominent and appealing college. The trustees, President Young, and President Lambert all agreed that Elon required a stronger athletic program—for greater regional visibility, to look more like colleges such as Furman or Williams, and to accommodate the more actively inclined, high-spirited, and adventurous students Elon was now serving. In the past decade, in addition to building the stadium, Elon has renovated the

Koury Center (for basketball and volleyball), the East Gym, Latham Baseball Park, and the softball field (for women's fast-pitch softball) and has installed an eight-lane, all-weather Olympic-quality running track. The athletic facilities are now among the best collegiate athletic plants in the East. The athletic budget has increased from $2.2 million in 1996–97 to $5.5 million in 2002–3.

In the early 1990s Elon left the National Association of Intercollegiate Athletics (NAIA) to join the better-known National Collegiate Athletic Association (NCAA) Division II. But soon after, the trustees authorized a study to find out whether Elon should go still further and enter the highly competitive NCAA Division I. After two years of study, the board of trustees approved the move, and in the fall of 1999 Elon became a member of NCAA-I. These moves enabled the university to increase the number of its athletic scholarships from 67 to 140 in the past six years in order to compete in seven men's sports and nine women's sports; teaching loads of the coaches were reduced to enable them to do more recruiting.

Ever ambitious, Elon's leaders yearned to move from their athletic conference to one that included the teams from colleges and universities that had greater admissions and academic overlap. President Lambert and Director of Athletics White especially wanted to join the Southern Conference, which included more well-known schools, such as Davidson, Furman, Wofford, The Citadel, the College of Charleston, and the University of North Carolina at Greensboro. The two men visited nine of the schools in the Southern Conference to lobby for entry. Then, suddenly, Virginia Military Institute, or VMI, the famous greenhouse for growing military leaders, decided to leave the Southern Conference. Elon was chosen to replace VMI and began playing the teams of the more academically oriented colleges and universities in 2003. "This was an important step for us to be associated with these colleges," says Provost Francis.

Along the way to greater athletic prowess, Elon encountered a problem that at first stirred considerable controversy. The school's athletic teams had always been known as the Fighting Christians because of Elon's religious origins. But the expanded admissions recruiting of the 1990s had brought onto campus a more diverse assembly of students. President Lambert says that he got calls from some Jewish parents objecting to the appellation Fighting Christians, and numerous Christian students, including some athletes, were also uncomfortable with the tagline. So Lambert consulted with all the constituencies, particularly the older alumni. There were objections to a name change, even a firestorm in one or two quarters. But the president persisted, and the Elon teams since 1999 have been called the Phoenix. A *phoenix* is both a desert bird in Egyptian mythology that was consumed by fire but then rose miraculously from the ashes, like Elon from its 1923 fire, and a person or thing of unsurpassed excellence, a paragon. Director of Athletics White explains that "the change was opposed by some, and a few claimed they would never give the college another dime. But after it was done, I received very little mail." A typical reaction was that of one of Elon's distinguished former athletes, Dr. Deborah Yow-Bowden, '74, now director of athletics at the University of Maryland and one of intercollegiate sports' top-ranking female executives:

I was angered at first by the name change. I remembered the small classes and scrappy teams and wanted to keep Elon as it was. But I realized soon that the name change was necessary.

A problem was how to pay for the university's high aspirations in the athletic realm. After all, Elon had too small an endowment for its appetite for growth and stature. Since 1973 the college had had a small Fighting Christian Club, but in 1997 college leaders established the Elon Athletic Foundation, with a full-time fund-raiser in the office of institutional advancement. The new booster club has helped obtain several major gifts, and in 2001–2 the foundation raised $350,000 for the sports program. Most of the students seem to appreciate the increased emphasis on athletics; many of them have been and continue to be active in an amazing array of recreational ventures. There are club teams in lacrosse, rugby (including women's rugby), horseback riding, ultimate Frisbee, and volleyball, among others, and each year groups go whitewater rafting on the Lower New River in West Virginia, rock climbing on Pilot Mountain, or kayaking along the North Carolina coast.

Attention to the growth and even jubilation of its students has become a deeply ingrained tradition at Elon.

Student Life and Pleasures

🐝 🐝 🐝

RICHARD HOOD is an associate professor of English
at Denison University in Ohio, an expert in and per-
former of old-time American country music, and a nov-
elist. But from 1987 to 1990, he was a young faculty member at Elon College, where he won the Sears Roebuck
Foundation Award for Teaching Excellence and Campus
Leadership. He remembers Elon as an institution that
worked its faculty very hard, that lacked a traditional
tenure system, and that included few important scholars or researchers:

> I loved my years at Elon. The college had two features
> that many colleges claim but few practice. One was an
> unusually warm, friendly community among the fac-
> ulty and administrators. The other was a genuine care
> for students and their growth. It's no exaggeration to
> say that numerous faculty loved their students. I still
> correspond with a few of my former students.

Elon has changed in many ways since 1990, but it has fought to retain its concentration on the intellectual and social development of students. It does so through an extraordinary range of actions, initiatives, requirements, and celebrations.

From a prospective student's first inquiry to Elon, he or she is treated with consummate courtesy. Several parents and students report that every telephone call, letter, or e-mail they sent was answered promptly and politely by obviously well-trained admissions and financial aid staff members. Visitors to the campus are given a tour by students who are said to be well informed and personable. Other colleges have similar programs, of course. But Elon adds some nice supplements.

One example is the Fellows Competition Weekend in early March. Students who are competing for merit scholarships such as the Honors Fellowships, Elon College Fellowships, Jefferson-Pilot Business Fellowships, Journalism and Communication Fellowships, and Leadership Fellowships flock to the campus to meet with faculty and Elon students who are currently holding fellowships. In 2003 more than four hundred came for interviews, a class, a seminar, and informational exchanges. The weekend is such an affable affair that 30 percent of the applicants who lose in the competition usually enroll at Elon nonetheless.

The orientation for new students is handled in large part by ninety juniors and seniors, whose twelve leaders have had three weeks of "preservice" training at Seven Lakes Retreat, a rural center owned by the university. The orientation group also teaches, along with faculty members, in the popular freshman seminar titled Elon 101, which is an all-purpose introduction to life at Elon: its academics, organizations, fraternities and sororities, athletic teams, library, residence hall relationships, and service opportunities. The Elon 101 faculty instructors also serve as students' adviser-mentors until they choose a major, usually in the sophomore year.

Elon's introduction to college life is so nurturing and welcoming that John Gardner's Policy Center on the First Year of College, at Brevard College, selected Elon in 2002 as one of America's Institutions of Excellence in the First College Year, and Elon's first-year program was praised by *Time* magazine in its 2002 Colleges of the Year issue. About 84–86 percent of new students return annually for their sophomore year, only a tad below the retention rate of America's finest primarily undergraduate institutions. Most students who leave Elon report in their exit interviews that the chief reason was homesickness, lack of adequate finances, or dissatisfaction with Elon's location. (The town of Elon is tiny, and its short main street adjacent to the campus lacks such amenities as a drug store, an emporium for books and CDs, a clothing shop, and an excellent restaurant.) Few departees complain about the teachers, fellow students, or campus programs.

Recruiting the Tyros

Throughout Fred Young's presidency, the admissions operation was a central concern, and it remains so under Leo Lambert's regime. The increase in applications to enroll at Elon is testimony to the success of the admissions effort, which has been a major factor in Elon's climb.

The university's admissions program does not do anything radically different from what is done at other leading schools. Rather, it has shaped a slightly different and highly competitive program of recruitment. The admissions and financial aid office is larger than most of those at peer institutions—twenty-eight persons, including officers and support staff. One-third of the staff travels a great deal, calling on schools and annually opening up new territories. When I asked about how Elon's recruiting differs, the answers were several. Elon spends more to create striking admissions materials; both the admissions view book and the video about life and study at Elon have won awards from the Council for Advancement and Support of Education. Former director Nan Perkins claims that "we probably send potential students more pieces of information than most institutions." Elon, like others, has two major on-campus open houses for parents and prospects, but at Elon many faculty attend and lead discussions. Twice a year guidance counselors from many states are invited to the university to inspect the campus; meet the students, faculty, and staff; and learn about the programs.

The admissions staff hold receptions each year in more than thirty cities, and a few students, professors, and parents are always on hand to talk to parents and prospective students. Dean of Admissions Susan Klopman explains that "we use parents more than alumni in recruiting. They are wonderful." Elon's responses to all inquiries are swift. Admissions officers buy geodemographic research to find out where the kind of students they seek are located, and they buy mailing lists from the College Board. There is great attention to getting the details right. "We try to exceed parent and student expectations at every step in the process," says one officer.

Why do parents and students decide on Elon as the place to study? Klopman claims that there is no one factor. Rather, most applicants like the size of Elon (not too small or too big), the attractiveness of the campus and facilities, the emphasis on dedicated teaching and student growth, the small-town atmosphere and moderate · North Carolina climate, the Elon Experiences and athletic teams, and the chance to study abroad and do internships. What especially capture many prospects, the officers say, are two things. One is the comparatively low cost of attending Elon. "It is equal to a $6,000 scholarship at more expensive-competitors," one person said. The other is the almost ubiquitous friendship and warmth of Elon's people. According to a staff person: "Lots of colleges tell people how friendly and welcoming they are. We really walk the talk."

In the past few years, the admissions crew has had to deal with the explosion in the use of the Web to look at colleges and a sudden increase in e-mails and on-line applications. Klopman says that "the Web has made a great difference. Admissions has become more consumer-driven." Elon seems to have responded quickly to the new approach by many secondary school students to searching for the right college or university with high-tech equipment.

Houses for Learners

In collegiate circles these days, there is growing talk about the need for "student-centered learning," presumably to replace the prevalent faculty-centered instruction, course calendars, and desires. Because of former president Young's attentions and Elon's underendowed condition, Elon has put students first for more than two decades. The leaders built an athletic building, a fitness center, a beautiful campus, and a lovely, large student center before they raised money for an enlarged modern library and an up-to-date science building. The students have benefited from ten new residence halls on campus and a commons building in a complex called the Danieley Center, named after the former president, and the older dormitories of Carolina, Smith, and West have been renovated. All living quarters are wired to the computer network.

Because numerous students requested them, Elon has instituted seven living-learning centers in the residence halls, where students with similar academic interests (such as creative art, science, or global studies) can live together. The university built six new fraternity and sorority houses in the past five years, with each Greek house run by a student manager, who also watches over the ten to twelve students who live in each house. About one-third of Elon's students belong to one of the nineteen Greek communities, seven of which are African American in membership.

The latest additions for student housing are two pavilions, the first buildings of President Lambert's intended "academic village"—a large Palladio-like villa (for classrooms) flanked by a series of smaller pavilions encompassing a grassy quadrangle. Similar to Thomas Jefferson's original design for the University of Virginia, the columned Georgian buildings are frankly imitative. As President Lambert has written,

> We like Jefferson's vision of interpreting the world in a small village, expressed in a distinctly American classical style . . . Elon's Academic Village pays tribute to Jefferson's design.

The first two pavilions, the Isabella Cannon International Studies Pavilion and the William R. Kenan Honors Pavilion, house twenty-two foreign students and twenty-two honors students. There are also a resident faculty member and classrooms in each pavilion. Jeffrey Stein, assistant dean of students, asserts that "the array of living accommodations at Elon is amazing and provides a maximum of choices for our students."

Many of Elon's publications are designed to be appealing to students, who are believed to be more bewitched these days by images and typography that spill over and splash colorfully, with bursts of copy. The printed pieces that Elon sends out to describe its programs and special features are replete with the boosterism typical of such promotional materials in higher education. But they are unusually well written and full of useful facts and wonderful action photographs that convey a sense of the energy of Elon student life. Jackson, vice president of student life, says: "Elon's students are exceptionally active. They start four or five new student organizations every year."

Because students today grow up with television, a computer, and the Internet, Elon has created a Web site that is one of the deepest, more visually stimulating, and informative among American colleges and universities. Dan Anderson, the reserved and thoughtfully innovative director of university relations, explains:

> We've merged our news operation and the Web. We've hired three experts, and they might change the contents of the Web page ten times a day. Students look at it regularly to find out what's going on, and some parents tell me they look at www.elon.edu nearly every day.

Celebrations and Involvements

Elon's chaplain, the Reverend Richard McBride, has been at the school since 1984. His commitment as Elon's spiritual leader is to help each student grow in mind, service, and spirit and to encourage each undergraduate to gain a clearer sense of self. Helping students transform and find themselves is part of what he calls "my own spiritual journey" and one of the main tasks of a collegiate chaplain in today's multiethnic and multireligious setting at most colleges.

Thus, in 1995 he started a "Turning 21" ceremony at Elon. Four times a year those seniors who turn twenty-one years of age are invited to a birthday dinner. Each young woman or man who accepts attends with a faculty or staff sponsor, who prepares a letter about how the student has changed while at Elon and what the sponsor hopes for the student's future. The letters are given to students at the dinner. About sixty students accept the invitation each time. Seated at round tables of eight each, the students are introduced by their sponsor, and then after dinner, students at each table offer a toast—to their teachers, the university, parents, friends, or the future.

McBride also teaches each spring a course titled Life Stories, which has become quite popular. In the seminar, students recall the factors that shaped them to become the persons they are and define what they hope to accomplish in the future. The students read books such as Don McAdams's *Stories We Live By* and Sam Keen's *Fire in the Belly* and are questioned by other students about their direction, habits, values, and more. Students report that the course really helps them discover who they are, how they became who they are, what they value, what their future might look like, and what steps they need to take to get there. In addition, McBride is editing the book *How Students Change in College,* which is being produced by fourteen students at Elon's Enterprise Academy, a creation of an associate professor of business administration, Barth Strempek, who helps students start small businesses in such enterprises as CD production, market research, and book publishing.

Elon bustles with celebrative dinners, retreats, committees, leadership roles, and events that feature students. Smith Jackson claims that "we take very seriously the empowerment of every student." An Elite Program has senior students who are expert at computer programming instructing faculty members in the possible uses of computers in pedagogy. Student government officers maintain a "Piddly List" of student suggestions about how to better life and learning at Elon, which is helpful during the annual retreat each August bringing together student leaders and top officers at the institution. Musically, there is a student-community orchestra, a chorale, and a jazz combo that tours. The current rage is a cappella singing groups. Several years ago students started Twisted Measure, a fifteen-person coed group that performs popular and entertaining songs. Elon's women have recently formed their own group, Sweet Signatures, which prompted the men to form MSG (Male Singing Group).

Assistant Professor of Political Science Dr. Sharon Spray started the Elon University Poll to engage political science students in citizen surveys and polling techniques. She designs the surveys, but students do all the telephone interviews. Spray sees it "as a tool for policy making." The students canvass North Carolinians about current state and national issues. The Elon Poll has become modestly influential and has been cited by such media as the *New York Times*, the *Wall Street Journal*, and NBC News.

And then there are the five Elon Experiences.

Engaging the Students

The latest Elon plan states that the institution seeks "to be a national model of engaged learning." The core of the university's effort toward this goal are the five Elon Experiences. They have been designed to promote the values that college leaders think are essential for young Americans to embrace and practice.

To develop a productive work ethic and help put knowledge into action, one experience is through internships and co-ops, arranged through the Career Center or the academic departments. About three-quarters of all students intern at organizations and business firms such as Merrill Lynch, the ACLU, the White House's chief of staff, NBC sports, Comedy Central, Johnson & Johnson, and the U.S. Information Agency. One student, Michael Hazel, reported, "My three internships—at Burlington Industries, the U.S. Open golf tournament, and Elon's admissions office—sharpened my interpersonal skills and taught me how to work in a team environment."

To inculcate an ethic of service, a second Elon Experience is service learning, which is coordinated through the Kernodle Center for Service Learning. Roughly 85 percent of each senior class has worked in one or more service roles, including such activities as blood drives on campus, building a house for the poor in the Dominican Republic or Alabama, tutoring Spanish-speaking migrants, and feeding homeless people in Washington, D.C.

Previous president Fred Young was a staunch propo-
nent of travel abroad to help students climb out of provin-
cialism and discover the amazing cultural, religious, and
linguistic diversity in the world. President Lambert
agrees. So the third of the five Elon Experiences is study
abroad. Today Elon has one of the nation's highest percentages of undergraduates who travel to and reside in a
foreign country, for one month to one year. About 62 percent of all seniors have had one such experience. Many
students travel during the winter intersession in a short
course, accompanied by a faculty member and often a
staff member as well.

People expect that those young men and women who
have more than ordinary intelligence and talent will later
use their gifts in leadership positions in government,
the arts, business, or other areas. Elon's executives and
faculty contend that smaller colleges, not huge universities, are ideal domains in which to learn and test leadership skills. So a fourth Elon Experience is to hold a leadership position in a student organization or participate
in the Isabella Cannon Leadership Program. In that program freshmen learn about themselves (their strengths
and weaknesses, values, and deepest feelings) and study
leadership styles. As sophomores they learn how to collaborate, build partnerships, manage conflict, and organize teams. During the next year, learning how to change
the status quo is central, while the fourth year is devoted
to practicing leadership—in campus organizations or
teams, in organizing events, and in training others to lead
or serve. More than half of all Elon seniors have held at
least one leadership position before they graduate.

Of course, a central value at any good college is the
pursuit of knowledge and the discovery of new knowl-

edge. To foster that, the newest and fastest-growing Elon Experience is undergraduate research, where students work with a faculty member or independently on research projects. More than three hundred students now annually make presentations of their research, and twenty or so present papers each year at the National Conference on Undergraduate Research.

Monitoring the Clientele

The early work of Lela Faye Rich prompted Elon's leaders and faculty to study their students in a more systematic and comprehensive manner. The annual surveys done by UCLA of new college students across the nation, called the Cooperative Institutional Research Project, or CIRP, disclose the attitudes, preferences, and values of freshman enrollees collectively and by institution. Elon's leaders study these survey results to get an indication of the views of new students nationally and of Elon's freshmen. An additional annual freshmen survey developed by the Policy Center on the First Year of College has also been used to get a look at those choosing to enroll at Elon.

The university surveys the entire student body annually about their satisfactions and dissatisfactions with life and study at Elon and often makes improvements based on criticisms or suggestions in the surveys. Of special importance are the Senior Satisfaction Surveys, where graduating students reflect on their years at Elon and its pluses and minuses. Even parents of the enrolled students are encouraged to make suggestions to improve the students' experiences. For instance, recommendations from the Parents Council have resulted in improved health and counseling services, guaranteed housing for sophomores and additional apartments for upperclass students, and shuttle services to the local airports during university break periods. The Elon surveys are executed and reported by Robert Springer, the relatively new director of institutional research, who is now trying to combine all the surveys to provide a sharper profile of the students and their life at Elon. Springer explains that

> Elon's officers are unusually interested in receiving information about the students and their views and academic progress. And they seem eager to share the data with everyone on campus.

From Their Mouths

What do the students at Elon think of the university's extraordinary attentions to their minds, well-being, and growth in character? To listen to them in focus groups or in stray conversations is a peculiar experience. Unlike interviews with undergraduates at most other colleges, Elon student reports are overwhelmingly positive. A few even border on the ecstatic. A skeptic might argue that critical thinking and dissent are undernourished at Elon. But most of Elon's students seem aware that they live, work, and study in a rather special place. They call it the "Elon Bubble."

By that they mean that they have somehow stumbled into a kind of Shangri-la, a weird but pleasurable little bubble of bliss, where they are treated like young adults; where they are the center of attention for some very smart and caring scholars, trustees, and staff members; and where professors really teach with skill and dedication. Here's a sample of comments taken from focus groups and casual talks with Elon students.

"It's incredible. The faculty and top brass actually consult students on every important issue."

"The biology classes are really intimate, and we get into research."

"The town of Elon sucks. But life on campus is so lively, the location doesn't matter that much."

"I like the idea that general studies requirements go through the senior year."

"We sit on nearly every committee—except tenure and promotions."

"Our professors tug us into expressing our own views and speaking in class."

"I can't get over how student-oriented this college is."

"One female sociologist who took us on some research abroad has actually won body-building contests."

"They even have a smoothies bar in the student center."

"Some of the teachers are a bit boring, but most are terrific."

"Even my coach seems to care about me and my future."

One parent I interviewed said that his son begged to return to Elon for a fifth year to study in another major. To an outside observer this all sounds unreal, rehearsed. But there does seem to be a kind of "Elon Bubble" of contentment and occasional bursts of outright joy.

Recognition Comes

Several years ago Dr. George Kuh, a professor of higher education at Indiana University and an authority on student affairs at U.S. colleges and universities, organized, with the help of others and money from two foundations, an instrument called the National Survey of Student Engagement (NSSE). The survey attempted to find out from enrolled students what they thought about their educational experience. The researchers chose five measures that they believed contributed to superior undergraduate learning: tough academic challenges, active and collaborative learning (discussions and presentations in class, team projects, volunteerism), close and frequent exchanges with faculty, other educational experiences (internships, study abroad, conversation with students of different color, ethnicity, and economic background), and a "supportive campus environment." They surveyed about 140,000 students at more than six hundred colleges and universities, and they continue to do so annually.

In every one of the five assessment areas, the students at Elon consistently report a higher percentage of satisfaction and positive activity than the NSSE average. And last year, for the third year in a row, Elon scored in the top 10 percent of the nation's colleges and universities in what NSSE survey designers call "engaged student learning." To the researchers undergraduate study consists of far more than taking notes at lectures and visiting professors' offices at rare scheduled occasions; instead, it prods students to become energetic and research-oriented scholars and community and professional leaders through a wide variety of educational activities and close and caring assistance from faculty members. Nearly 95 percent of Elon's students consistently rate their education as excellent or good in the annual surveys.

Clearly, Elon has succeeded in developing a large cohort of pleased student consumers. There seems to be a markedly small amount of cynicism and a great deal of enthusiasm among Elon's undergraduates, who evidently recognize that their university is deeply committed to their progress as learners and persons of character.

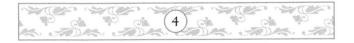

Elevating the Academics

P RESIDENT LAMBERT and his staff talk continually
about Elon becoming "a national model of excellence
in engaged learning." There can be little doubt that the
institution is close to being one of America's exemplary
student-oriented colleges. Most professors teach diligently, travel with students abroad, and work closely
and often with students on research projects, committees, and enterprises. But until recently few would have
claimed that Elon is a fountain of important scholarship.
While the faculty's preoccupation with student growth
has been helping students stretch their minds and sen-
sibilities, the teachers have not had much time for, nor
have they been pressed much to engage in, research and
path-breaking scholarship. As late as the mid-1990s, not
a single Elon faculty member had a sponsored research
grant, though several had received small grants for improving courses, curriculum, and teaching techniques.

But since 1999 and the arrival of Dr. Lambert, Elon
has gradually introduced new measures to expand the

scholarship of the faculty and increase the intellectual opportunities for and demands on the students. Lambert is determined but prudent. As he says, "Elon does not move by radical shifts. We open the valves slowly."

Actually, efforts to improve the intellectual climate at Elon began during the later years of President Young's administration. The college revived its tradition of bringing major speakers to campus and has long had an academic honor code. In the late 1990s Elon reduced faculty teaching loads from four courses a semester to three and raised faculty salaries. A new science building and an ultramodern library were planned to encourage more research and aid better scholarship. More students with high academic credentials were being recruited each year.

A key person in raising academic accomplishments in the late 1990s was Dr. Rosalind Reichard, then dean of the sciences division. She sparked the founding of the Undergraduate Research Forum in 1996, and two years later undergraduate research was added as a fifth Elon Experience. Reichard helped design the McMichael Science Center and introduced a new series of lectures in 1998 called "The Voices of Discovery." In this program, innovators in scientific discovery such as Stephen Jay Gould, Nobel Laureate William Phillips, and Jane Goodall spend a day with students and then deliver a lecture on their work in the evening. Nancy Harris, a biologist who is now associate dean of Elon's College of Arts and Sciences, is only one of several to say that Rosalind Reichard was a major force in improving Elon's academic climate: "She was widely respected. Many of us were sorry to see her leave for the academic vice presidency at another college."

In early 1998, just after President Young announced

his retirement, the vice president for academic affairs, Julianne Maher, organized six working groups to study parts of Elon's intellectual climate for an "Academic Summit" on April 4, 1998. Its purpose: to assess the current academic climate and to suggest ways "to enhance the intellectual climate." The faculty members, students, and staff persons at the summit pretty much agreed that "the Elon culture fosters social interaction over intellectual challenge" and that many students tended to "overcommit to out-of-class activities" and slight their class assignments and serious scholarly investigations. The summit participants proposed several changes, such as increasing academic rigor and challenges, giving more awards and greater recognition for intellectual achievement, hiring more full-time faculty, and increasing the "overlap of social and intellectual activities." Conspicuously missing from the final document was any mention of the need for increased scholarship and research by the professors themselves. Published scholarship by most of the faculty was thin, as the annual dean's reports of faculty publication and grants before 1999 testify.

Opening the Valves

Soon after Lambert arrived in 1999, however, it became clear that, while enthusiastically admiring the active and experiential teaching and learning that had made Elon regionally more distinctive, he saw the need to deepen and expand the scholarship and research of the faculty and provide enlarged support and recognition for intellectual and artistic achievements. He launched a multipronged offensive. Lambert believes that "hiring new faculty members is the most important decision an institution makes." He and Provost Francis have hired nearly sixty new faculty members in the past four years, mostly at the assistant professor level, shunning the fad of hiring big-name senior professors for collegiate window dressing.

The screening of new faculty candidates at Elon is very thorough. Each prospect must teach a class, engage in scrutiny sessions with students and future departmental colleagues, and present a description of her or his scholarly interests and work to the faculty. This process is not unusual. What is unusual is how Elon orients, guides, and assists each faculty appointee. New instructors begin with a week-long orientation to Elon and then continue to attend monthly orientation sessions. Each is assigned a senior faculty mentor to assist with his or her new life at Elon and to sharpen teaching skills. Deans, other academics, and administrators invite the novices to lunch. Monies have been set aside for summertime travel and research by new faculty members, and Lambert has raised funds for something he calls "emerging scholar professorships" for those who appear to have exceptional promise in their pretenure years.

An Elon faculty committee prepared a paper on "The Elon Teacher-Scholar," which is overly rhetorical and full of academic bromides but makes the point that, while excellent teaching is central at Elon, significant scholarship should accompany everyone's classroom instruction. Provost Gerry Francis claims that "we take scholarship more seriously now." As the former chair of the trustees, Wallace Chandler, '49, says, "Our emphasis now is on academic improvement."

Some of the new faculty appointments have already quickened the intellectual and artistic activity at Elon. Catherine McNeela, who had spent years in professional theater, has rapidly given Elon a program in musical theater that is suddenly being touted by some as one of the better ones in America. During one of my visits, a highly talented admissions applicant from Singapore was being auditioned for the musical theater program. Richard D'Amato started an innovative one-person program in pre-engineering at Elon and has initiated 3-2 transfer arrangements with five major universities. D'Amato believes that engineering students today tend to "lack manual dexterity," so he has his students do projects such as constructing a canoe from cardboard and plastic garbage bags that will float on the campus lake. Elizabeth Rogers, a national leader in training programs for physical therapy, has established Elon's only doctoral program—in physical therapy. (Physical therapists will be expected to have doctorates by 2020.) Her dean claims:

> She's fantastic and has brought in superb associate faculty. Her new program received CAPTE approval without a single criticism, for the first time in CAPTE's history of evaluations.

Michael Skube, a Pulitzer Prize winner for criticism, has joined the growing faculty in communication. Heidi Glaesel Frontani, a geographer who speaks Swahili, is an often-published expert on world water resources and fisheries. Elon has also sought out promising new African American scholar-teachers such as Linda Poulson in accounting and finance professor Joseph Meredith, the son of James Meredith, the first black student admitted to the University of Mississippi.

For the existing faculty at Elon, the number of sabbaticals has increased; money for faculty research grants, travel to conferences, and new course design has expanded. There are new endowed professorships, such as the J. Earl Danieley Chair held by sociologist Thomas Hendricks, an authority on play and emotional satisfaction in contemporary life, and the Maude Sharpe Powell Professorships, held by philosopher and longtime faculty member John Sullivan and English professor Russell Gill. The acquisitions budget for the Belk Library has tripled since 1999. Faculty are encouraged to study abroad with students in tow. A special suite of rooms was set aside on campus to become El Centro de Español, a center for instruction in spoken Spanish, open to students, staff, and faculty. It is directed by a language teacher from Costa Rica, who hopes to teach more persons at Elon to speak Spanish as well as English.

Gerald Whittington, the vice president of business, finance, and technology, contends that

> hiring is the most important thing we do. Good programs and excellent facilities are all critical. But the special culture of Elon is our comparative advantage, and the right people are essential to preserve that culture.

Restructuring the College

When Leo Lambert assumed the presidency in January 1999, he found an Elon College that was composed of five undergraduate divisions with the Martha and Spencer Love School of Business attached. He noticed that the largest enrollment for major study outside the business school was in the Department of Communication and Journalism, and he often heard the Department of Education referred to as "the ed school." So he floated the idea of creating separate schools of communications and of education alongside the Love School of Business and consolidating the arts and sciences into a liberal arts college. Thus, Elon College would become Elon University—a name for which several trustees had lobbied—composed of an arts and sciences college (to retain the name of Elon College) and three professional schools: business, communications, and education. After some heated and emotional campus discussion, fragments of it strongly oppositional, and advice from consultant Edwin Wilson, provost of Wake Forest University, Elon College became Elon University on June 1, 2001.

While the idea of changing Elon's name from college to university was being discussed, Lambert and Provost Francis petitioned for membership in a recently formed small group of institutions called the Associated New American Colleges, or ANAC. The consortium was the early 1990s brainchild of the late Frank Wong, then vice president of academic affairs at the University of Redlands in California, who was devoted to creating a more practical and contemporary liberal arts education. Wong advocated a mix of some professional training, some research, and some community or regional service with the traditional liberal arts courses, unlike the "pure" liberal arts education of, say, a Reed, Carleton, or Swarthmore. In 1995 the late Ernest Boyer, president of the Carnegie Foundation for the Advancement of Teaching, was captivated by the concept of a new layer of American academic institutions that were not research universities, exclusively undergraduate liberal arts colleges, or career-oriented state colleges and universities. Boyer invited Wong's little group to Princeton, New Jersey, to help organize the ANAC.

The ANAC institutions are medium-sized (3,000 to 7,000 students) and are devoted to a core liberal arts education combined with preprofessional or professional studies and service opportunities. The ethos is student centered, not faculty centered, and faculty are expected to be dedicated to expert teaching as well as to scholarship and research. The goal is to turn out graduates who have a historically grounded and applied competence, not just theoretical knowledge, young women and men who can use knowledge for constructive action and wise policy making in society.

Lambert and Francis thought that ANAC's aims were remarkably close to what Elon was already doing, so Elon applied to join, and in March 2000 Elon was selected for membership in the group, which is now composed of twenty institutions, including Valparaiso, Hamline, Susquehanna, Dayton, Hampton, and, of course, the University of Redlands. The North Carolina school issued a news release shortly after joining:

> Elon, and the other ANAC schools, are advancing a third kind of educational model for American higher education . . . Our strength lies in a strong liberal arts foundation for all undergraduates, interwoven with outstanding professional programs in a collegial and student-focused campus environment.

A two-year study by a distinguished panel and the resulting 2002 report of the Association of American Colleges and Universities, titled "Greater Expectations: A New Vision of Learning," advocated that more colleges become like the ANAC twenty because higher education in America requires more than small, elite liberal arts colleges, large, research-rich universities, and vocationally oriented institutions:

The panel calls for a new national commitment to provide an excellent liberal education to all students, not just those attending elite institutions . . . Professional studies—such as business, education, health sciences, technologies—should also be approached as liberal education.

In this spirit, the report urges an end to the traditional, artificial distinctions between liberal and practical education. Liberal education in all fields will have the strongest impact when studies look beyond the classroom to the world's major questions, asking students to apply their developing analytical skills and ethical judgment to significant problems . . . By valuing cooperative as well as individual performance, diversity as a resource for learning, real solutions to unscripted problems, and creativity as well as critical thinking, this newly pragmatic liberal education will both prepare students for a dynamic economy and build civic capacity at home and abroad. (p. xii)

Planning for the Coming Decades

Planning during President Young's years had become an indispensable guide for setting priorities and making decisions at Elon, an approach strongly supported by several of the trustees. And most people on campus thought the 1994 strategic plan called the Elon Vision was a highly useful blueprint. But by 1998 it was largely fulfilled. It seemed inevitable that, soon after Lambert took office in January 1999, he and the trustees would hatch a fresh strategy of action for the first decade of the twenty-first century. As Noel Allen, chair of the trustees, says, "We are always looking around the corner."

What the new president pushed into motion, however, took some people's breath away. He initiated three different plans, more or less concurrently, between 1999 and 2000. One was the Elon Vision for Technology of 1999. This three-year plan began soon after Lambert arrived, with workshops to help faculty integrate technology into their instruction with the aid of an outside consulting group. The plan, adopted by the trustees in October 1999, called for improved administrative computing, wiring all campus buildings, increasing the staff to assist with academic uses of computers, wireless laptops in Belk Library, a three-year replacement schedule for new computers, and the establishment of a Technology Center on campus so that everyone could stay abreast of the latest advances in electronic hardware and software.

Elon recognized that it had been slow to adopt the possibilities of the new communications technology for educational uses, and it spent and raced to catch up. It still lacks a CIO (chief information officer), and some faculty remain reluctant to incorporate high-tech methods into their classroom teaching, though students have more than adequate resources for computer use on campus. One outside evaluator of Elon's technology recently charged that, while Elon has introduced all sorts of technology for the students, staff, and faculty, the institution, like many other colleges, has not yet found a way to restructure its education to capture the benefits of the communications revolution:

> The information technology effort needs to become more closely linked and integral to the educational mission of the University . . . Elon needs someone dedicated to the integration of the information technology vision into the fabric of the University.

The second planning thrust was for an updated facilities master plan. The university had continued to grow
in enrollment, and it was running out of classrooms.
Also, some older buildings needed renovations, several
new buildings seemed imperative, and some outdoor
spaces needed to be reconceived. Elon sought a master
planning firm that could figure out how Elon could
expand while retaining the attractiveness of its 575-acre
campus.

Elon hired the architectural firm of Spillman Farmer
in Bethlehem, Pennsylvania, which had some previous
experience with the university. The firm had worked at
Atlanta's Agnes Scott College when financial vice president Whittington had served there and had done outstanding work at nearly a dozen smaller private colleges,
from Lake Forest College in Illinois to Susquehanna University near their office. Hiring Spillman Farmer turned
out to be an act of serendipity. As Robert Spillman told
me, "Our style is to do lots of listening with all the key
groups and individuals before we start our campus master plans. We learn from them. And obtaining buy-in for
our plan is vital." He and his planning partner Dan Harrigan interviewed widely, sketched possible designs (Harrigan, a former champion swimmer, is an exceptional
sketch artist), and produced a master plan that is a combination of novel and bold ideas and conservative designs.
It attempts to maintain the snug community life and
focus on student growth that Elon espouses.

Spillman says that his work at Elon "was one of the
most satisfying jobs of my career." He cited the readiness of many persons to offer fresh suggestions, the quality of the leadership, and the transparent concern for students and their quality of life. The Academic Village is one

of the firm's bolder ideas, one that President Lambert eagerly adopted. The master plan also proposed several other additions and moves: a location for the proposed new business school building and an inn for conferences, sites for additional residence halls and a large convocation center, and the conversion of a former large grocery store and lot just west of the campus for the new home of the physical plant staff and printing shop. Architect Spillman also recommended that Elon's academic leaders work with the town's political leaders to develop an attractive downtown shopping area adjacent to the campus, create a new entrance to the university from the new bypass road north of the campus, and undertake renovations to the Jordan Center, a cluster of old residence halls.

The master plan was received favorably, though the site for the new Koury Business School building has lately been moved. Spillman Farmer is not a firm that features flamboyant Frank Gehry–like structures but is sensitive to keeping the scale, building materials, fenestration, and external appearance of new buildings close to the already existing architecture and visage of the campus.

At the same time as the plans for new technology and physical plant were gestating, the university's officers, faculty, students, and staff were meeting to construct a new strategic plan, to be called the NewCentury@Elon. The planning team was characteristically ambitious.

New Directions for Tomorrow

Uncharacteristically, however, the strategic plan that emerged in late 2000 was a scattershot, effusive document, containing seven objectives and forty-five initiatives. It mixed operational improvements and genuine strategic priorities and left out references to technology and its possible new uses. It called for five new buildings: for the business school, student residences, a new visual arts building, a health center, and a convocation center to be used for such events as basketball and indoor graduations. It suggested a new running track and additional renovations. As for programs, it urged an improved core curriculum and honors program, a more active career planning office and public relations offensive, and enlarged graduate programs.

The first draft of NewCentury@Elon also called for three new academic centers (for environmental studies, international studies, and innovative teaching and learning), an institute for policy and public affairs, and a whole new school of information technology. There were lots of calls for new monies, of course, to endow the schools of education and communications and the newly created arts and sciences school, Elon College; to endow more professorships and student scholarships; to increase faculty salaries and provide more sabbaticals for the professors; and to aid in financing student travel abroad. To accomplish all this, the planners advocated a more aggressive and skillful program of fund-raising, one that would raise the surprisingly low alumni giving to 40 percent and double Elon's endowment. NewCentury@Elon also wanted the School of Business and the School of Communications to obtain national professional school accreditation, and it hoped that student participation in public service, internships, and study abroad would all increase.

The plan that emerged from the planning group, headed by Trustee Noel Allen, would have required more than $250 million in new funds and seemed to lack focus or clear priorities. An astute commentator on Elon's forthright Self-Study of February 2002 for the Southern Association of Colleges and Schools (SACS) asked:

Where is Elon headed? Will progress and greater recognition mean that it becomes more like other institutions, or will it remain distinctively Elon? . . . Is there a unique path for this University, and if so, how will the institution define it? . . . What should a stronger Elon be?

Sensing that the planning team of 2000 may have wandered from the reservation, top Elon officials and faculty decided to accept many of the planning group's strategic initiatives but recast the final strategic plan into just three goals and fewer initiatives. Most importantly, they brought greater focus to the plan by concentrating heavily on improvements in academic quality and scholarly activity. They also incorporated a few ideas from the technology and facilities plans and added one important new quest, the pursuit of a Phi Beta Kappa chapter, and one questionable one, a law school. A revised strategic plan, titled "NewCentury@Elon: A Blueprint for Excellence," was issued as a spiral-bound booklet nearly two years later, in 2002.

The three goals were simple: increase academic excellence, provide new facilities to help boost Elon's academic life, and gather the resources to make the next steps possible. But underneath the goals was a sturdy commitment to raising the level of scholarship and research at Elon in the coming decades. This, the strategic plan urged, would be done by reconstructing the honors program; increasing spending on the library, student fellowships, and technology; attracting more faculty who showed strong scholarly promise; deepening the learning component of the five Elon Experiences; and gaining professional accreditation for the new School of Communications and the older Love School of Business. Most noticeable, though, was a recommendation, prompted in large part by President Lambert's predilection for strengthening the so-called liberal arts (history, English, biology and chemistry, mathematics, political science, music, philosophy, economics, psychology, and classical and religious studies), to make Elon "a university with arts and sciences at the center." To do this, the plan introduced two ideas not in the first draft of NewCentury@Elon.

One was the construction of the academic village that architect Spillman had suggested to house the liberal arts faculty and to provide more up-to-date classrooms for their instruction. The other was to pursue a Phi Beta Kappa chapter and join the ranks of the 270 noted institutions that have been admitted to this intellectual U.S. fraternity. In a curious sentence buried in the copy, the blueprint also read, "The Board of Trustees has authorized a feasibility study for the establishment of a school of law." The second and third goals—facilities for excellence and more financial resources—were similar to the initiatives proposed by the original planning group, with some specifics dropped and others added in the new resources section.

Wasting No Time

In the past few years, Elon University has rushed to implement the revised NewCentury plan even as it was being crafted. The flurry of initiatives to lift the level of intellectual discourse and intensity of study has been awesome. The Honors Program, headed by chemistry professor Dan Wright, has been reduced in size and made more rigorous; forty Honors Scholarships have been created, providing a minimum of $9,500 in merit-based aid; and a striking Honors Pavilion has been built in the Academic Village to house twenty-two of the selected students. The Phi Beta Kappa quest has been launched, led by Russell Gill, a professor of English, who has his work cut out for him because only 40 percent of Elon's current students are interested in majoring in the liberal arts and just 10 percent of Elon's faculty are members of Phi Beta Kappa themselves. But President Lambert has created thirty-five new Elon College scholarships for those who intend to major in the sciences, humanities, social studies, or arts. Gill says the university will apply in 2003 but admits that it will be a tough and probably long process to attain Phi Beta Kappa status. To him, "The journey toward Phi Beta Kappa status will be beneficial to Elon even if we don't get accepted quickly."

Additional funds have been allocated to bring renowned leaders and arts groups to the campus. Elon students and faculty have heard and met such political leaders as Israel's Ehud Barak, Poland's Lech Walesa, South Africa's Nobel Laureate Desmond Tutu, Costa Rica's Oscar Arias, Pakistan's Benazir Bhutto, and former president George Bush; such writers as David McCullough, Doris Kearns Goodwin, and David Halberstam; such art groups as the Shanghai Ballet and London's New Vic Theatre; and film maker Spike Lee. Elon has put fifteen five-week courses on-line for summer learning. The average freshman SAT scores have risen from 1085 five years ago to 1150 in 2002–3, and SATs almost certainly will continue to increase as the achievements of Elon become better known. Statistics was just added as a core requirement for all students not preparing for work in the sciences or engineering.

Each of the university's four schools—business, education, communications, and Elon College, the arts and sciences school—has been working busily to raise itself into greater intellectual regard. At the School of Business, Dean John Burbridge is planning for an AACSB (Association to Advance Collegiate Schools of Business) accreditation visit in February 2004. Worried because the business program is not regarded as among Elon's strongest academic areas, Dr. Burbridge brought in two sets of outside reviewers. Both recommended that the school's faculty needed to engage in more scholarship and research and that the school required a stronger faculty that could make intellectual contributions to the fields of economics, management, and accounting and finance, the school's three divisions. President Lambert promptly provided Dean Burbridge with three additional faculty positions; the dean hired a total of eleven new faculty members between 2001 and 2003. The business school is being scrubbed and transformed.

The School of Education is already accredited and has a record of turning out sought-after teachers. Graduates have been recognized as Teachers of the Year at local and state levels. The 1987 National Teacher of the Year was an Elon alumnus. And Elon is one of only two private institutions in North Carolina selected to participate in the North Carolina Teaching Fellows program, a competitive honors program that provides students with $13,000 scholarships. The reserved Dean F. Gerald Dillashaw says: "Our program is very field-based. So we have a tension between great teaching and the new demands for more research and scholarship."

The School of Communications has magnificent new quarters in the McEwen Building, the former library. The interior was renovated in bright colors and has a perky quality unlike the more prim and dignified interiors elsewhere on campus. The school also has a relatively new dean, Paul Parsons, a balding, charming, candid, highly articulate Midwesterner: "I feel I've come to heaven. Every faculty member in our school is a winner." With 850 majors, communications is the most popular academic concentration on campus. The students produce an excellent weekly newspaper, operate an FM radio station, and work with the faculty on biweekly television news and magazine shows. As preparation for the upcoming accreditation visit, Dean Parsons spent eighteen months with his faculty revising the school's curriculum, which was instituted in 2003. It stresses the content of ideas and information over technology and engineering, emphasizes good writing and speech, requires a practical internship of every major, and demands that students take eighty hours of credit outside the school, preferably in the arts and sciences. The new curriculum has four concentrations: journalism, broadcast and new media, corporate communications, and cinema.

Dean Steven House of Elon College, the recently reassembled arts and science college, is also new. A physiologist who has taught at Columbia University and Seton Hall University, he is the most extroverted and youthfully eager of the four deans, who go to lunch together every Wednesday. Fascinated by Elon's approach of engaged learning, House is also hopeful that he can stimulate more faculty to be productive scholars.

Elon's professors seem to have received the message that the next decade is to be one of enhancing the academic reputation of the university. The annual reports on faculty achievements from 2000 to the present reveal an outpouring of scholarly articles and poems, new grants for research, papers presented at scholarly conferences, and some five to eight books a year now being published by Elon University's 235 or so full-time faculty. Intellectual and artistic ferment seems to be taking its place alongside attention to student growth as a distinctive feature of Elon University.

Financing the Rise

🌱 🌱 🌱

A QUESTION that is often asked is: How could Elon University, with a pitiful little endowment and a tuition lower than that of similar schools, rise so fast from being a so-so college to one that is attracting national attention and increasing applications? With so little money and no huge benefactors, how was Elon able to transform itself so rapidly? How on earth did they pull it off?

The university performed this quasi miracle by using more than a dozen different measures. But many at the university attribute a large portion of the achievement to one person, the fifty-four-year-old vice president for business, finance, and technology, Gerald Whittington. Several persons at Elon use adjectives such as "ingenious," "unbelievably canny," and "cautiously daring." The former chair of the board of trustees, Wallace Chandler, believes that "Gerry is one of the best financial vice presidents in American higher education."

At a February 2003 faculty meeting, Whittington was

asked to explain whether there would be cutbacks because of the recession, the depressed stock market for Elon's investments, and the university's increased expenditures for student scholarships and faculty salaries (which went up a whopping 10% in 2002, to the fourth highest among the state's private institutions after Duke, Wake Forest, and Davidson). Whittington admitted that there would be some pinching here and there but explained in detail how Elon's finances remained solid. When he finished, the faculty rose and gave him a standing ovation! Not many financial vice presidents in academe receive such outbursts of acclaim.

Whittington, who had an itinerant youth because he is the son of a military family, attended college at the University of North Carolina at Chapel Hill, where he surprisingly took elective courses in music and voice training. (He is an accomplished lyric baritone, and to this day he participates in about fifteen concerts a year.) After receiving an M.B.A. from Duke, he entered the special world of higher education finance and accounting. He became a vice president at the 600-student Agnes Scott College in Atlanta's suburbs at the early age of thirty-four. By 1991 he was ready for larger challenges, and he heard about an opening at Elon. He applied and was chosen vice president on January 1, 1992. At the time Elon College had 3,227 students, an operating budget of $32.5 million, and a meager endowment of less than $14 million.

Unperturbed, Whittington went to work modernizing everything from the administrative computer system to the way the college's endowment was invested. He strongly supported President Young's dream of making Elon one of the better colleges in the East but worried that the college had very few affluent alumni, having graduated many teachers, clergy, and midlevel businesspersons over the years. He knew that the trustees were generous and dedicated but not abundantly wealthy. On top of that, most of the college's leaders and trustees in 1992 were uncomfortable with borrowing more money to finance Elon's liftoff.

Whittington also observed, however, that Young had repositioned the college and was pressing the admissions staff to bring in more students from affluent families throughout the eastern states. Whittington seized on this as an opportunity to improve the finances of the institution. He supported the initiative to invest heavily in the admissions office and urged the admissions staff to work hard to "grow" the enrollment by adding 100 to 110 new students a year. At the same time, he pressed to hold the discount rate—the tuition dollars returned to entering students as scholarships—at only 12 percent, thus compelling the admissions office to entice more students with little or no financial need to study at Elon. Most other private colleges and universities were returning in financial aid to students 25, 35, or even 45 percent of their sticker price tuition, receiving only 75, 65, or 55 cents of income for each dollar in tuition revenue.

The admissions dean, Nan Perkins, and her staff performed admirably, and every year since 1996 Elon's enrollment has increased by about one hundred students, providing the college with $1 million in extra income, the equivalent of interest on $20 to $25 million of endowment income. Today more than two-thirds of the parents of Elon's students have incomes of $75,000 or more, and fewer than 10 percent of the undergraduates estimate their parents' income at less than $40,000, compared with roughly 30 percent of all American college students.

Since Elon could not dispense many scholarships, Whittington and his colleagues decided that the college's tuition should be kept as low as possible, both to help Elon's parents pay their college bills and to make attendance at Elon seem a good value. As of 2002–3, Elon's cost for tuition, room, and board was $20,400, 6 percent less than that at comparable colleges in the South and 35 percent less than better private colleges in New England. Elon is currently listed in *Barron's Best Buys in College* as one of the 280 "best buys" in undergraduate education. As Whittington explains:

> At the heart of our financial strategy were three things: growing the enrollment gradually, strict control of tuition discounts, and a competitive, value-oriented tuition price.

Bricks, Mortar, and Loans

But if Elon was to recruit more students from prosperous families, the campus had to provide a vastly improved infrastructure, the basic facilities and services for the functioning of a desirable college community. To satisfy this need, Elon's leaders believed they had to do two things. One was to continue President Young's drive to create and maintain a beautiful, up-to-date campus. The other was to persuade the trustees to borrow a great deal of money to build, as quickly as possible, state-of-the-art new facilities for the increasingly bourgeois clientele and to launch simultaneously a capital campaign for bricks and mortar and for an enlarged endowment.

Whittington began to borrow millions of dollars, much of it in tax-exempt bonds with a variable rate of interest. By 2003 Elon University had accumulated $54 million in debt, a perilously large amount for an institution with a 2003–4 operating budget of $90 million. This is a debt–to–operating budget ratio of 60 percent. To help pay for the debt, he and the trustees decided to set aside 4.5 percent of the budget each year as cash reserves for debt service. According to Whittington:

> To some, such heavy borrowing may seem imprudent. But Elon needed huge sums to deliver on its ambitions. We've built, renovated, and leased twenty-seven buildings in the past decade. And today [2003] our variable interest rate is less than 1 percent!

In little more than a decade, Elon has become one of the nation's loveliest and best-equipped small universities, mainly by attracting larger enrollments, holding down financial aid, and borrowing boldly.

Of course, there were other contributing factors. The capital campaign of 1996–2001 amassed $47.6 million, thanks to some large and many generous gifts from alumni, trustees, parents, and friends. The amazing rise in stock market valuations in the late 1990s helped the endowment grow. The Elon faculty and staff were willing to accept comparatively modest salaries during the college's offensive to build the infrastructure for a first-rate small university. Elon also benefited from its location between Durham–Chapel Hill and Greensboro, enabling the university to hire excellent and less costly adjunct and part-time faculty. While the number of Elon's full-time faculty has grown in the decade 1994–2003 from 140 to 235, the school has continued to employ 60 to 70 adjunct instructors annually, now about 28 percent of the total teaching force.

Whittington also squeezed dollars from every sector

of Elon's operations and gathered new dollars from such innovations as issuing a Phoenix Card, debit and credit, from which the school earns a percentage, and granting Coca-Cola exclusive "pouring rights" for soft drinks on campus for a fee. Thus, he somehow always seems to have modest funds to invest in new ideas, improvements, and repairs (such as the replacement of campus trees damaged or killed by North Carolina's winter ice storms). For example, some of the "pouring rights" income is used to finance a one-week trip to London each year for selected staff (including custodians, secretaries, carpenters, and electricians) and faculty to show the university's appreciation for their work at the institution and to connect with Elon's study abroad program.

A close examination of Elon's finances turns up dozens of cost-saving frugalities. Working with the trustees' investment committee, Whittington has diversified the investment of Elon's endowment by placing it with two bond firms and four different high-quality stock houses. The stock market's sharp decline from 2000 to 2003 cost some U.S. colleges and universities about 20 percent of their endowment—Wake Forest's endowment, for example, plunged 24.4 percent in the two years between 2000 and 2002—but Elon's endowment has dipped only 5.7 percent, primarily because Elon has invested equally in value, growth, and core stocks and well-selected bonds. Elon's average annual return for the past ten years has been 10.8 percent. "We invest for the long run and resist tinkering to increase short-term gains," says Whittington.

Elon University's administration is comparatively lean, and staff salaries are slightly lower than those at most peer colleges. President Leo Lambert in 2001–2 earned $263,207 in total compensation, which is comparable to the compensation of presidents at Furman University, Roanoke College, and Washington & Lee but below the total compensation of the president of competitor Rollins College in Florida ($324,243) and the president at Alabama's Birmingham-Southern College ($357,335). Several of the administrative staff also teach occasionally. Gerald Whittington regularly teaches a one-semester course in finance at the business school; Smith Jackson co-teaches a seminar in the psychology of student development; student dean Jeff Stein, a poet, teaches a course in creative writing; and Chaplain McBride teaches his Life Stories class.

Until 2002, the salaries of Elon's 235 faculty were also slightly lower than those at most similar institutions. And in hiring new teacher-scholars, the university's leaders have almost exclusively appointed young assistant professors and shunned the hiring of expensive senior and big-name scholars. The cost savings of this tactic are considerable. Whittington asserts that "the academic officers are the most important budget managers on a campus, not us financial folks."

Purchasing is another area in which Elon has excelled. Without resorting to the cheapest items, the university's business staff has artfully managed to acquire most items, from food to computers, at bargain prices. Recently, the National Association of Education Buyers named Elon as one of the top ten nonprofit purchasers in the nation.

See-Through Budgets

The budgets of many U.S. colleges and universities are arcane. Neither the process of deciding on the budget, its size, and its allotments nor the amount of many of the appropriations in the budget is known to most persons on campus. Not so at Elon. The budgeting process is remarkably transparent.

It begins in the fall of each year with Vice Presidents Whittington and Francis looking at the present year's operations, Elon's NewCentury strategic plan, and the local and national financial picture and then roughly shaping the budget for the next academic year in approximate outline. They then take it to President Lambert for confirmation or alterations. Next, the proposed budget outline with its priorities is shown to the executive committee of the board of trustees, who approve it or suggest some changes. This done, the budget committee, composed of Whittington, Francis, and one elected member of the faculty, draw up guidelines for all academic department chairs and staff division heads to assist them in preparing their own budget presentations for the next year. The guidelines include such items as the inflation rate, admissions and retention data, and the overall financial picture. Then each department head prepares her or his requested budget, based on the guidelines, and presents it to one of the four deans or a vice president. These requests are trimmed or increased in places, and a rough first cut of the upcoming budget is sculpted.

In January the rough first cut, along with its operating assumptions and reasons for new monies, shifts in resources, or continuing allotments, is presented at an all-campus forum. Not just faculty but everyone who works at Elon is invited. Questions are asked, and some community members offer suggestions for changes in the proposed budget. "Are we budgeting enough for computer training?" "How adequate is our funding to aid travel-study abroad?" "Why are we not renovating the dorms this year?" After this the budget committee whittles, adds, and rearranges once more, and a few weeks later they bring the revised proposed budget to the all-university forum again for further questions, suggestions, and final comments.

This revised and tweaked budget for the next academic year then is shown to the president for further possible minor adjustments before going to the board of trustees for final approval. According to Whittington, the trustees have altered the proposed budget only once in the past decade "to increase the amount we had allocated to faculty and staff salaries."

Budget making at Elon is viewed not only as a way of parceling out scarce monies but also as a way of educating everyone in the Elon community about how much is being spent and how and why it is being spent. The process is also viewed, at least by Whittington, as a means for receiving criticisms and innovative suggestions in advance from those who must live within the budget's financial boundaries.

Coming Soon: A New Financial Strategy

Two of the cornerstones of Elon's financial strategy have been annual growth in admissions and a very low discount rate in financial aid. Both are now being challenged.

The Elon Vision of the late 1990s suggested that, to stay a friendly, vibrant, cooperative community, Elon should not grow beyond four thousand students. By 2003, however, Elon had enrolled 4,432 students, and some faculty and students were beginning to think that the university was growing too big, especially since it was now splintered into four separate schools and there was talk of more graduate students and perhaps a new law school.

Also, Elon's strategy to capture maximum tuition revenue was to limit tuition discounting to a mere 12 percent. But President Lambert's desire to increase the quality of Elon's entering students had prompted him to establish numerous new merit scholarships for the brightest applicants and to undergird the strengthened Honors Program. The initiatives have forced Elon's discount rate to jump from 12 percent to 17 percent in 2003–4, an increase of 42 percent. The university has also increased faculty salaries considerably.

Thus, two of the building blocks of Elon's financial strategy that have enabled the university to build rapidly and grow in stature despite its small endowment are in jeopardy. Whittington responds this way:

> We'll still continue to grow. Only we will probably grow twenty or thirty students a year instead of one hundred. And it is important that Elon continues to increase the quality of its students through the use of merit awards in the face of a very competitive climate for the brightest and best. But there is no question that we will need to create a new financial plan.

Elon has already begun to rearrange the derivation of new monies to help the university maintain the momentum of its ascent into the highest ranks of America's institutions of higher education. Elon's officers and trustees have been budgeting more heavily for Nan Perkins's Office of Institutional Advancement, increasing its resources by nearly 50 percent. She has hired new experts in corporate giving and in deferred giving and wills, and she plans to create an enlarged cadre of volunteers to assist in gathering gifts "to increase peer-to-peer solicitations."

Fund raising at Elon has been heavily dependent on a

relatively few alumni, friends, parents, and trustees. Now the university's officers will need to spread their nets to foundations and corporations and encourage many more people to include Elon in their estate plans. They intend also to increase the annual contributions of Elon's graduates, who have thus far been disinclined to return donations in significant percentages or amounts for the attention they received at the college.

Despite occasional successes, the fund-raising operation at Elon has never quite developed the consistent superior performance exhibited by other operations at the university. A leading Elon officer explains, "We've had some leadership and personnel problems there over the years, and until recently fund raising has not had the priority and investment it now has." But the future growth of Elon depends increasingly on the professionalism and energy of the development staff. The university cannot borrow much more, and student tuition revenues will grow more slowly. Nan Perkins and her staff have become a linchpin, as she and her other staff were for admissions during the 1990s.

Almost certainly, the four deans will be expected in the future to aid in gathering new monies. Whittington realizes that "we'll probably need to slow the spread of new programs, too, and concentrate more intensively on what we do really well." With the cost of higher education, like the cost of health care, growing 30–40 percent a year faster than the U.S. Consumer Price Index, Elon will undoubtedly be required to keep scrambling, scrounging, and strategizing.

The university's leaders have become uneasy, but they remain resolute about further enhancing Elon's standing. In 2003, President Lambert and the trustees approved the purchase of an eighty-acre stretch of land across the railroad tracks to the south of the campus. It had been occupied for decades by the Elon Home for Children, a private sanctuary for orphans and troubled youth. The cost was $2.8 million. According to Whittington:

> We're not sure what we will do with the land and its houses. But Elon is still growing, and we wanted to protect the beautiful campus. Besides, surfers need to keep ahead of the next wave.

This is another big investment for a university with a relatively small endowment of only $55 million. But Elon is an institution that has gambled shrewdly and seems likely to continue to do so.

6

The Fruits and Ironies of Success

❦ ❦ ❦

THE TRANSFORMATION of Elon University over the past two decades has not gone unnoticed. Elon has climbed a few levels every recent year in annual appraisals by *U.S. News & World Report* and is now rated as eighth among master's level southern universities. *Barron's* ranks Elon as one of the 280 "best buys" in college education. *The Templeton Guide* identifies Elon as one of the top one hundred U.S. colleges and universities in the "character development" of its students. In the *Kaplan Day Star Guide to Colleges for African American Students,* Elon is named as one of one hundred best schools in the nation for black students. *Yahoo Internet Life* magazine selected Elon as one of the top one hundred wired colleges. Elon has been cited as having one of the best freshman year programs. And, in the National Survey of Student Engagement, Elon has scored in the highest 10 percent of the nation's colleges and universities three years in a row for having an educational program and climate that challenge and engage students to an extraordinary extent.

When *Washington Post* education reporter and Harvard graduate Jay Mathews published his 2003 book *Harvard Schmarvard,* he wanted to get beyond the institutions that had big reputations and find the "lesser-known jewels." His probing and unscientific survey placed Elon first on a list of one hundred lesser-known gems that, according to guidance counselors and others, deserve greater national attention. Elon University has undoubtedly become a "hot" little university.

All the planning, planting, and strategic nurturing by Elon's leaders have clearly borne some fine fruit. The number of applications keeps increasing. Exceptional young faculty who wish to teach as well as do scholarly work are increasingly attracted to the school. New and larger gifts are now beginning to be showered on the university. And the reputation of some of Elon's academic programs has begun to swell. In fact, a few persons who study undergraduate education in America are convinced that Elon has become a paragon among U.S. colleges. One example is John Gardner, the executive director of the Policy Center on the First Year of College, located at Brevard College in western North Carolina:

> To me Elon is the new gold standard for undergraduate instruction in America. They do almost everything right. Every officer, professor, and staff member seems courteous, informative, and caring. Elon is a real community, and one that is becoming quite scholarly. I've given them one piece of advice: "Don't screw it up!"

The Consequences of Success

The meteoric rise of Elon into the ranks of the country's finest undergraduate institutions has, however, begun to reveal some ironic results. This is not unusual. When an institution surmounts its crippling problems, or attains new fame for its extraordinary accomplishments, or triumphs in its strategic efforts, the institution almost always encounters unexpected new predicaments. Success, especially rapid success, comes at a price.

Similarly, initiatives in one desirable area often collide with laudable innovations in another area. Communities, societies, and universities are not naturally harmonious; they are inevitably full of incompatibilities and differences. An example is the rush by colleges to incorporate all the latest digital technology into their operations and style of information exchanges. The new electronic communication vehicles have, of course, enormous benefits. But what if a college prides itself on face-to-face exchanges between diverse students and maximum contact between students and their professors? Are simulations as enriching as personal, direct experiences with people, ideas, and predicaments? Both swift and efficient computerized on-screen exchanges and warmer, more friendly personal exchanges are desirable in academe. Both seem to enhance learning. But are they compatible?

Elon has begun to uncover some ironic consequences of its success and to bump into its own little incompatibilities. Fortunately, the school is assiduously introspective. More than one executive and faculty member told me, "We have a healthy paranoia." Elon's Institutional Self-study, prepared for the accreditation visit of the Southern Association of Colleges and Schools, displays an unusual candor and a refreshing sense of the university's shortcomings.

Take the growth in enrollment during the past decade. The faculty, campus leaders, and many students and alumni not long ago thought that Elon would lose much of its gregarious, highly valued, and mutually helpful sense of community if enrollments rose above four thousand students. Yet today Elon's enrollment is nearly forty-five hundred and still growing. In addition, there are discussions about increasing the number of graduate students and programs. At what size does community feeling begin to crack, divide, and erode?

Partially because Elon's financial aid situation has been pinched, Elon's students are overwhelmingly Caucasian and fairly affluent. The university has made considerable effort to increase the number of African American undergraduates, who now constitute about 8 percent of the enrollment. But neither Hispanics nor Asians make up even 1 percent of the student body, even though these two groups will soon constitute nearly 20 percent of the U.S. population. Also, only 1.6 percent of the students report being Jewish. President Lambert has added an additional full-time multicultural recruiter to the admissions office, and a recent $3 million gift has been set aside to endow, each year, eight Watson Scholars—North Carolina students who come from low-income families.

Given the increasingly polyglot nature of America's population and the continuing inflow of Hispanics, Africans, and Asians into the United States, Elon certainly needs to reach for greater ethnic diversity, especially among Latinos and Asians. But might a powerful move toward broad student heterogeneity result in the creation of ethnic enclaves and divisions among the students, as has happened at numerous other campuses, thus contributing to a possible loss of Elon's cherished "Elon Bubble"?

Will Elon's entry into Division I athletics, with its increase in athletic scholarships, pull the school into becoming a university with a growing number of "jocks," or young athletes primarily keen on excellence in their sport rather than in their studies? How, at the same time that it expands its athletic prowess, can Elon be seeking more of the academically gifted young for each freshman class with its abundant merit-based fellowships? Isn't it incompatible to attract more athletically able students, who must remain on campus to practice and play their schedule of games, while advocating—even requiring— more students to go off campus to work in internships and to study abroad?

The Really Big Tension

Elon's rapid ascent in academic stature is principally based on the school's laserlike focus on student growth, with an active and engaged approach to learning, com-prehensive student involvement in university policy mak-ing, skillful and devoted teaching, and a supportive envi-ronment that includes close advising and a country-club campus setting. Adherence to this approach to under-graduate learning at Elon seems widespread and deep. It is rooted in Elon's urgent need to attract and satisfy students in the 1980s and 1990s; in the college's reli-gious origins, which fostered education for values, ser-vice, and soul-searching as well as for intellectual growth; and in the kind of students that Elon enrolled. The com-mitment is still palpable.

But now that Elon has begun to gain some national attention and acclaim, its leaders, especially President Lambert, many faculty, and the trustees think that the university should become a more scholarly place. So Elon has launched a drive to increase its level of intellectual and artistic accomplishments, with more faculty expected to do research and publish in major journals and more students going on to graduate school and earning Ph.D.s. Major attention is being given to an improved Honors Program and the Honors Fellows. Dozens of new merit-based fellowships have been created to attract more of the nation's academically gifted students. Tenure procedures have been altered to include more scholarly achievements. Professional accreditation is being sought for the schools of communication and business.

The recent drive to gain intellectual distinction as well as praise for attention to student needs and transformation is not just a desire to further enhance Elon's prestige. In the past decade Elon, with its energetic, action-oriented students, has been drifting away from study of the arts and sciences toward becoming more of a professional and quasi-vocational university. Between 1997 and 2003 the percentage of students earning an undergraduate degree in the arts and sciences (arts, biology, chemistry, English, history, mathematics, music, political science, philosophy, psychology, and the like) declined more than 10 percent. Undergraduate interest in business, communication, education, engineering, film making, human services, leisure/sport management, public administration, and theater has grown during the past five years. One disgruntled faculty member was quoted in Elon's 2002 Institutional Self-study:

> As Elon College becomes a comprehensive university, it is losing its commitment to its historic liberal arts core as the focus of undergraduate education. The liberal arts and humanities have been marginalized at Elon.

The drift away from the liberal arts and toward professional and preprofessional training has prompted President Lambert and his colleagues to find ways to reinvigorate the "centrality" of the liberal arts at Elon. Two of Lambert's moves have been to create a new academic village for the arts and sciences college and to apply for a Phi Beta Kappa chapter. PBK membership is heavily dependent on an institution's steadfast dedication to the traditional liberal arts and to profound intellectual inquiry. PBK leaders tend to look askance at professional training and perhaps "engaged learning" for undergraduates. But both Lambert and Professor of English Russell Gill, who is spearheading the school's quest for PBK, claim that the journey toward Phi Beta Kappa status will be therapeutic and is necessary to ensure a better balance in Elon's undergraduate education.

In the decade 1994–2003, Elon students' ability to perform more rigorous academic work and Elon's emphasis on the liberal arts have gradually increased. The mean Scholastic Aptitude Test (SAT) scores of the freshman class have increased from 1040 in 1994 to 1159 in 2003, and the students' high school grade point average (GPA) has risen from 3.1 to 3.6. Six-year graduation rates have jumped from 63.2 to 71.2 percent, and more Elon graduates now go on to graduate and professional schools, about 18 percent immediately after college and an estimated 20 percent more after one to three years of travel or work. These figures are considerably below those at the finest liberal arts colleges and excellent smaller universities, but the direction is promising.

Elon's emphasis on active learning, work, and community service produces many graduates—about 43 percent—who have two or even three job offers by the end of their last college year, frequently as a result of their summer jobs, co-op positions, or foreign travel. For instance, Annie Reilly, '03, who interned with two area newspapers and a communications firm during college, started as an assistant editor of United Airlines' in-flight entertainment guide. Rich Bloomquist, '00, a writer for television's *Daily Show*, won an Emmy award for writing in 2003. Elon students seem to be moving toward more intellectual interests while at the same time moving more quickly into jobs and professional positions that match their abilities, interests, and kinetic energy.

Elon's efforts to complement its extraordinary focus on student growth, values, and self-scrutiny with a new and robust advance toward more traditional liberal arts education and faculty research and scholarship, and with a press toward making its three professional schools as powerful as any in the Southeast, have created a new kind of tension on campus. Time is always the scarce resource. Most students will probably experience greater difficulty finding enough hours for personal experimentation and socializing, for more intensive academic study, and for preparation for some form of postgraduate work and service. And many faculty will increasingly be torn between fervent teaching and assistance with student growth and heavier responsibilities for scholarship, publication, and academic distinction in their fields.

According to one of the outside consultants who commented on Elon's arts and science section of its 2002 self-study, after interviewing numerous faculty members:

> Many faculty members feel a "culture of busyness" that claims all their time and leaves them without opportunities for research or for growth and renewal. They fear that greater attention to research will require less cre-

ativity in the classroom, less breadth in their own reading and learning, and restricted availability to students.

Can Elon remain one of the foremost student-oriented,
user-friendly colleges in the land and also become an
incubator for innovative scholarship and professional
education?

Dueling with the Dilemma

On a Friday afternoon and Saturday morning in late November 2002, President Lambert held one of his Leadership Elon sessions, as he now does several times a year.
A mix of thirty-five to forty faculty, alumni, local resi-
dents, students, staff, and trustees are invited to each
session. The participants review the priorities of the New-
Century@Elon strategic plan and hear about the admissions picture, several faculty initiatives, the newest proposed facilities, and the finances of the university. At these
meetings they get to question the president about where
Elon is going and why and about how Elon hopes to get
there. Leadership Elon sessions are one of Lambert's
inventive means for keeping everyone informed about
current conditions and Elon's plans for the future and
for preserving the sense of community despite Elon's
growth. Lambert believes that "we have incredible team-
work at Elon. We play in each other's sandboxes and collaborate constantly."

Campus leaders seem fully aware of the fruits and the
increased stresses brought by success and innovations.
Leadership Elon is one of several measures developed in
an attempt to straddle such emerging conflicts as innovative student-oriented, engaged learning versus old-time
Phi Beta Kappa scholarship, contemplation, and empir-

ical studies, and earlier strategic priorities versus the new directions for Elon's future. Balance has become a major concern—between liberal arts and professional studies, teaching and scholarship, Lela Faye Rich's ENFP effervescent, action-oriented students and the increased number of highly studious merit scholarship winners, improved residential life and foreign travel and off-campus internships, and the development of intellect and the development of character and self-understanding.

This is a problem nearly as old as U.S. higher education. Are colleges largely to educate for knowledge accumulation or to produce citizens who understand their civilization's history and national heritage and their own potential and obligations? Should colleges prepare students primarily for life or for work? For pride in America's democratic society or for tolerance of the world's many different cultural, religious, and political forms? Should the best colleges become distinctive and special, or should they be balanced, multifaceted, and open to diverse student and faculty interests?

Elon has risen in many people's estimation as one of America's finer institutions for student-oriented undergraduate higher learning. The cry from many is something like "Don't screw it up!" But even the esteemed and exceedingly thoughtful President Lambert asks: "How do we stretch our goals? How do we sustain our momentum?" The answers are far from transparent. But he and Elon seem not to have lost their lust for further excellence.

7

Analysis of an Ascent

IT IS ALWAYS HAZARDOUS to draw principles from a single case. Yet the rapid rise of Elon College, now Elon University, from ordinariness, parochialism, and near-poverty to distinction, worldliness, and financial stability is perhaps worth a search to locate the factors that made the climb possible. The search may be helpful in some ways for colleges and universities that aspire to rise in quality and renown.

If one looks carefully at the actions of Elon in recent decades, six features that aided the college's ascent stand out. One is former President Fred Young's mantra of "quality everywhere." Dr. Young constantly preached that every aspect of Elon's operations should be excellent, and he labored to ensure that every event on campus, every trip abroad, every class of instruction, every telephone response was as courteous, clean, smooth, and helpful as possible. To this day, if you call any office or faculty member at Elon, you will almost certainly hear a friendly and informative voice. If you visit Elon, the grounds and plantings will be pristine and attractive to the senses. Before any new building is constructed, a contingent from Elon will have visited the best that other colleges have built so that Elon's structures have quality and appurtenances that approximate the finest elsewhere. The trustees forbid Elon's leaders from ever allowing needed maintenance to be deferred.

Of course, many other colleges and universities possess high-quality ingredients—in their programs of, say, music or computer science, in their student services, or in their handling of alumni. But few have worked so diligently as Elon at trying to make right every aspect of their institution's operations, from the food served on campus to the cleanliness of the college's washrooms. Elon exudes a sense of doing things right, of being well run. This is a feature that parents, visitors, consultants, students, and faculty notice and comment on very favorably.

A second feature is Elon's addiction to planning. Both President Young and President Lambert created strategic priorities, set goals, and, more importantly, communicated the next steps widely and made sure that the strategies were carried out and not allowed to become mere paper proposals. Elon's visionary strategies become action imperatives and targets for financial investment, with annual reports on the progress of each strategic plan. Moreover, the strategic plans are based on sagacious competitive analyses, making Elon distinctive and giving it a comparative advantage. Elon is not plain vanilla. The strategies are coupled with architectural master plans so that the physical and material requirements for strategic initiatives are in place.

Many U.S. institutions of higher education are risk averse. The reluctance of many faculty bodies and presidents to change, and especially to take daring leaps forward, is legendary. Not so at Elon. It is a risk-taking institution, willing to gamble that its adventurousness will pay off. Elon manifests a cautious self-confidence and collective faith, one based on keen analysis and shrewd appraisals of society's novel inclinations and emerging attributes. Elon's trustees, faculty, and executives boldly design their future; they do not allow it to drift pell-mell in response to outside events.

The Importance of People

Higher education is largely a people business. Much depends on the quality of the students, professors, trustees, and leaders and on the loyalty of the graduates. Elon University seems to recognize this reality. As the institution has risen in stature, it has become even more meticulous in its selection of new people at every level.

The third feature of Elon's advance, I think, is its attention to the selection, training, and rewarding of people. And Elon pays attention to all its people. At Leadership Elon meetings, planning sessions, budget presentations, and Tuesday morning breaks around the fountain, the invitees include grounds workers, secretaries, and security guards as well as professors, vice presidents, and students. Elon is one of the most inclusive communities in American higher education. Ever since the presidency of J. Earl Danieley (1958–73), who would not let the furor over the war in Vietnam, the civil rights upheaval, or student revolts and radical changes in dress, speech, and music disturb or divide Elon's community culture and dedication to teaching and learning, the university has valued its cooperative community life as a jewel-like possession. Vice President Whittington, no sentimentalist, calls this the "Elon way," with everyone unceremoniously urged to be polite, inclusive, information-sharing, service-oriented, and involved in Elon's progress.

New faculty and staff are selected as carefully as a great chef would select fish or vegetables at market. And they all receive orientations, training, and coaching. The student clientele is the result of targeted recruiting, the gentle wooing of high school guidance counselors, and the circumspect selection of fellowship and scholarship recipients. The selection of Leo Lambert to succeed Fred Young as president was likewise an exceedingly thorough process, and Lambert seems to be as determined and engaging a leader as his predecessor. Forceful and enterprising leadership from both the presidents and the trustees has propelled Elon into more estimable company.

Elon's harmonious, caressing community—the "Elon Bubble," as the students call it—has resulted in astonishingly little turnover among faculty and staff, despite comparatively low salaries before 2002 and comparatively taxing duties. Fred Young was president for twenty-five years, which one vice president says was "an incalculable asset. He provided a continuity, an unwavering purpose, and a sustained delivery on our strategic plan objectives that few other colleges ever enjoy." Gerald Francis, Nan Perkins, G. Smith Jackson, Lela Faye Rich, Susan Klopman, Gerald Whittington, Rev. Richard McBride, and Alan White are all executives who have been at Elon for a decade or more. And a majority of the faculty and trustees have also been attached to Elon for surprisingly long periods. This condition could easily lead to dry rot. But the energy, devotion, and commitment to progress of nearly all who have remained seem to be as staunch as ever.

By selecting students, faculty, and staff who are likely

to contribute to Elon's growth and cozy community life ("the Elon way"), Elon gains amity but denies itself the rich variety of people who can add spice to an institution's human and academic exchanges: the moody poet, the radical social scientist, the stern taskmaster scientist, the carping philosopher. Is a wide range of characters among students and faculty conducive to greater academic achievement and humorous alumni memories or to excessive disputation and the corrosion of purpose?

A fourth feature that has contributed to Elon's new prominence is its willingness to create a distinctive niche in the crowded firmament of American colleges and universities. Elon has for several decades pinned its hopes on an unusually strong devotion to student growth. It has assembled an array of devices to pull students out of adolescence, narcissism, and cupidity onto a higher plane of living. Elon's leaders proudly broadcast their powerful emphasis on "engaged learning," an action-oriented, experiential style of education that goes way beyond passively attending lectures, taking notes, gathering data from the Internet, and taking examinations.

To give muscle to the claim of engaged learning, Elon has insisted that each faculty member be a motivational, inspiring teacher, one who meets often with her or his students. The university developed the five Elon Experiences, and Elon involves students in nearly all policy deliberations. It helps arrange internships that inspire students to gain maturity and confidence. Courses like Wellness and Rev. McBride's Life Stories encourage students to know themselves and their values. The vibrant set of extracurricular and athletic activities helps, too, as does the recent increase in undergraduate research, which unites students with the more scholarly faculty.

Much of the curricular and extracurricular program at Elon is based on constant assessment of its students' characteristics. The fit between Elon's academic offerings and the kind of students who have been attracted to Elon is snug. The university's leaders may be a bit too boastful in believing that their peculiar style of engaged learning is the coming wave in undergraduate instruction, but thus far it seems a creative, productive, popular, and quite distinctive venture.

Financial Acumen and Marketing

The fifth feature of Elon's success is the school's acumen about financing growth with relatively small amounts of its own money. The presidents, advancement and financial officers, and trustees have been as strategic about borrowing, pricing, and soliciting new money as Gerald Francis and others have been about academic programs. Elon sets its tuition competitively, staying below the price of peer colleges, to convey a sense of value, of being a best buy. It cleverly devised an unusual admissions offensive and an extremely frugal discount rate not only to reposition the college but also to create a source of needed revenue. Then it borrowed money audaciously to help provide a campus environment as lovely and contemporary as any, aiming to please the strata of students it was enrolling.

Elon has been both daring and inventive and yet prudent and scrupulous. It has leveraged its limited funds with remarkable skill. Whittington says that "we try to get three dollars worth of results out of every two dollars we invest."

But now that President Lambert and school leaders are intent on lifting Elon to a new level of scholarship and academic renown, the financial situation is changing. Already Elon is carving out new financing priorities to cope with the continuing ambitions of the university.

The sixth and final feature that seems to have been helpful to Elon's rise is its recent skill at marketing. As old hands know, marketing consists of more than aggressive advertising and promotion. Promotion is just one of the five Ps of higher education marketing: program, price, place, people, and promotion. Elon believes that it has created an appropriate program of academic and extracurricular activities for its student market. Elon's price, or cost of tuition, room, and board, is kept competitively lower than that of most of its rivals. The place, or campus appearance and facilities, has been given devoted attention and investment, and Elon's people are chosen and trained well to be attentive to student and parent needs.

Elon, however, did not give much heed to promoting itself to the larger public until President Young's later years. But it has eagerly and deftly sought notice of its special traits and ballooning quality in the past decade. In 1994 a consultant was brought in, and in 1998 Elon hired Dan Anderson, a soft-spoken and modest but masterly ex-journalist, who has increasingly gathered plaudits and mentions for Elon. With a directive from President Lambert, Anderson has put in place a series of initiatives aimed at the news media, publishers of college guides, higher education leaders, and influential people in government and the nonprofit sector.

The admissions recruiting booklets and materials, already eye-catching, became even more visually alive and well written. Elon's alumni magazine became a quarterly, with lots of well-written news if not yet a tidy magazine design. Elon began sending an annual financial report not only to graduates but also to the presidents, top officers, and admissions directors of the 125 leading schools in the southern region. President Lambert asked Anderson to get Elon mentioned and known nationally. So he has visited the offices of several media and has invited higher education writers to the campus. Some of these contacts have resulted in stories in such journals as the *New York Times*, the *Washington Post, USA Today, Time* magazine, and the *Chronicle of Higher Education*. Anderson has paid less attention to television and radio because, as he says, "The power of print is still the greatest."

Bringing world-famous figures, from former president George Bush to broadcast legend Walter Cronkite, to campus has given students exposure to powerful notables and something to brag about at home, and it has made some very important visitors aware of little-known Elon University. The same goes for the scholars from around the country who have participated in "The Voices of Discovery" program. The Elon University Poll, run by students under the guidance of political scientist Sharon Spray, received considerable publicity during the resignation of Senator Jesse Helms, the senatorial race between Elizabeth Dole and Erskine Bowles, and the emergence of John Edwards as a U.S. presidential candidate. And the various college guides have obviously been informed about the "new" Elon, though Elon has not yet made it into *The Fiske Guide to Colleges*, an influential book that purports to describe America's "best" colleges and universities. The guide's editors, however, have just informed the university that Elon will be included in the 2005 edition.

Coda

Much has been written to criticize the management and hidebound nature of U.S. colleges and universities. For a majority of America's academic institutions, the charges have considerable validity. But a large minority of the nation's thirty-nine hundred homes of nonprofit higher learning have been busy and strategic in recasting themselves for the novel conditions of contemporary society and the world. Elon University is one of these and thus deserves scrutiny.

Also noteworthy is the stealthlike emergence of a new kind of American large college or small university. It is not a research university nor a highly intellectual, small, liberal arts college. Neither is it largely devoted to educating young persons for the world of work, as are many state colleges and universities and undercapitalized private colleges. It is unashamedly a hybrid, steeped in the liberal arts but connected to preparation in the major professions. This new kind of college or university recognizes that it will not attract many of America's most gifted students. Seventy percent of this small group chooses to go instead to the top twenty research universities and ten of the most elite liberal arts colleges. It also recognizes that many other students attend college largely in order to get a good job. The new hybrid college or university has chosen to educate the middle group, many of whom are moderately bright, talented, not yet fully committed to serious intellectual inquiry. This new tier of academic institutions has created a fresh menu of academic programs and requirements, a different structure of activities, and a more motivational and intimate pedagogy. It has also hired and oriented professors for a slightly un-conventional style of work.

This new kind of college or university is still inventing itself, still groping for the best way to educate the not quite brightest and best who prefer to be scholarly practitioners, entrepreneurs, and civic professionals. This quest results in a certain restlessness and a pull toward experiments and innovations, as well as a hankering for greater recognition for their sometimes unusual but extraordinary achievements.

Igor Stravinsky, the composer, is said to have remarked, "The great artist is the one who is always looking for the cool spot on the pillow." Elon University seems to possess that relentless restlessness. It is an institution that I find fascinating and believe is worth studying and watching.

Afterword

❦ ❦ ❦

The Last Decade?

Many of us who knew George Keller were deeply saddened by his passing in 2007. What a joy it would be to walk the Elon campus with George and talk about a decade of change since *Transforming a College* was published in 2004. I was delighted when George's editors at Johns Hopkins asked me to craft an afterword to update readers on the Elon story.

Many of the people in *Transforming a College* remain in place, and others have since retired. I am completing the fifteenth year of my presidency. Gerald Whittington, Smith Jackson, and Dan Anderson continue in their same roles. Provost Gerry Francis transitioned to the role of executive vice president after fifteen years of exemplary service, and Dean Steven House was appointed provost following a national search.

Younger team members have joined the senior staff of the university, including Jim Piatt, vice president for university advancement; Greg Zaiser, vice president for admissions and financial planning; and four others who were introduced to administration through the Faculty Administrative Fellows program, an opportunity for faculty with leadership promise to take on a significant administrative challenge and participate in the daily life of institutional leadership. In searching for high-level leaders, Elon has achieved a reasonable balance of cultivating talent internally and identifying new leaders through national searches. But there is no question in my mind that longstanding, talented, and committed leadership in the vice-presidential roles was essential to a smooth presidential transition early in my tenure and that new senior hires brought fresh perspectives and energy to my team.

Many other of the book's notable characters went on to receive the Elon Medallion, the university's highest award for service, including Nan Perkins, Susan Klopman, Alan White, Chaplain Emeritus Richard McBride, Lela Faye Rich, and Distinguished University Professor John Sullivan. President Emeritus Earl Danieley is approaching his ninetieth birthday and still teaching and tremendously active in day-to-day campus life. President Emeritus Fred Young resides near Pinehurst, North Carolina, and remains highly interested in the progress of the university.

Faculty and staff remain the heart and soul of the campus, whether full professor or gardener, dean or electrician. All are committed to creating an ideal environment for learning. I am reminded at our service recognition luncheons each spring, where faculty, staff, and administrators of all ranks come together to honor significant service anniversaries, that it takes each and every talent represented in the room to make the learning environment vibrant, safe, and smoothly functioning. The respect of my colleagues for each other's work is palpable.

Full-time faculty members have increased from 261 in 2004 to 394 today; they are joined by about eight hundred full-time staff members. The student-faculty ratio has improved from 14.9:1 in 2004 to 12.3:1 today.

Faithful adherence to strategic planning and careful execution of those plans remain important characteristics of Elon's institutional culture. Institutional priorities determined each year by a larger leadership circle will lead to progress toward strategic goals, and a senior staff member is assigned as responsible for leading each priority. In addition, the university budget committee, which has faculty and staff representation and is responsible for annual budget preparation, is guided by the strategic plan. These practices lead to effective follow-through on major institutional goals.

The NewCentury@Elon strategic plan detailed in this book was completed in 2009, with a concomitant launch of a new strategic plan, the Elon Commitment, in December 2009. The Elon Commitment was a collaboration of faculty, staff, students, alumni, and trustees and is organized around eight major themes: an unprecedented commitment to diversity and global engagement; supporting a world-class faculty and staff; attaining the highest levels of achievement across our academic programs; launching strategic and innovative pathways in undergraduate and graduate education; stewarding Elon's commitment to remain a best-value university; developing innovative alumni programs to advance and support the Elon graduate; establishing a national tournament tradition of athletics success along with the highest academic standards for Phoenix athletes; and significantly enhancing Elon's campus with premier new academic and residential facilities and a commitment to protecting our environment.

The university's endowment remains very modest compared to those of peer and aspirant institutions but, despite the crash of 2008, has grown from $57 million in 2004 to about $180 million today. The board of trustees resolved to make endowment fund raising the centerpiece of Ever Elon, a $100 million comprehensive campaign completed in 2011; approximately 60 percent of the funds were directed to the endowment, principally for student scholarship aid. Elon's alumni base remains exceedingly young, with 60 percent in their twenties and thirties.

Elon's board of trustees has been pivotal to the university's progress of the past decade. Extended board retreat weekends with faculty and staff guests in St. Petersburg, Florida, and in Highlands and Roaring Gap, North Carolina, have provided valuable opportunities for extended conversations about the university's future. I have been privileged to work with a string of enormously talented board chairs: the late Bob LaRose, Gail Lane, Noel Allen, Zac Walker, Jim Powell, Allen Gant, Mark Mahaffey, and Wes Elingburg. The executive leadership of the board has been scrupulous about setting agendas focused on the most critical strategic issues facing the campus, avoiding the common trap of having board meetings consist of presentations about already solved problems, and interacting with faculty, staff, and students as much as possible. Significantly, the board has transformed from principally a local board to a much more national one. In the Ever Elon campaign, co-chaired by Mark Mahaffey,

Allen Gant, and Kerrii Anderson, trustees contributed a generous 25 percent of the $107 million raised.

Parents continue to support the university with great generosity, contributing $1.32 for every dollar given by Elon alumni. The current and immediate past chairs of the board of trustees are former parents, and Elon parents serve on nearly every major board and council. An active and thoughtful Parents Council remains a vital force at Elon, and many members have adopted Elon as a second alma mater. Elon parents have been an essential force behind the institution's progress and success.

Another demographic shift of note that would interest George Keller is the increase of out-of-state enrollment to nearly 80 percent of Elon's student body, with 12 percent of the first-year class from Massachusetts alone. A 2013 research study by Prescience Associates shows a 49 percent growth in Elon's tertiary recruiting markets, with notable gains in California, Illinois, and Texas.

Elon receives nearly 10,000 applications today for an entering class size of 1,450, up from 8,000 applications in 2004. Significantly, 75 percent of deposited students report that Elon was their first-choice school. Elon's principal competitive set today includes both public institutions (e.g., University of North Carolina at Chapel Hill, James Madison University, North Carolina State University, University of South Carolina–Columbia, College of William & Mary, and University of Maryland–College Park) and private institutions (e.g., Duke University, Davidson College, Wake Forest University, Boston College, University of Richmond, and Syracuse University).

Despite the growth from fewer than four thousand students in 1999 to sixty-three hundred today, Elon is smaller than most of its competitors. Our market advantage is that we are a midsized institution with a broad array of both liberal arts and professional majors, while retaining the intimacy of small classes taught by engaging professors in an idyllic collegiate setting. In my judgment, there is no question that growth has been good for Elon, providing us with the necessary funding base to offer a more expansive curriculum, excellent faculty, top-tier experiential learning programs, and many other investments in quality. *U.S. News & World Report* ranked Elon as the #1 southern master's-level university (tied with Rollins College) in its 2014 guide, up from a #9 ranking in 2004.

The following is a brief synopsis of the development of Elon University since George Keller last told the story ten years ago. I hope this update adds to a good case study from which many institutions will benefit.

The Flourishing of Arts and Sciences

Elon University saw the achievement of one of the most important milestones in its history—the sheltering of a chapter of Phi Beta Kappa—in 2010. The North Carolina Eta chapter was formally installed at the Spring Convocation for Honors, following the dedication of Phi Beta Kappa Commons in the center of Elon's Academic Village.

Meeting Phi Beta Kappa's high academic standards took three applications over nine years. After the first denial, faculty and administrators visited John Churchill, secretary of the Phi Beta Kappa Society, to learn more about the qualities of institutions with successful chapters. A much more complete application was submitted three years later but was rejected, largely because Elon was still in the process of reinstituting a foreign language requirement that had been eliminated from the general studies curriculum thirty-five years earlier. Mr. Churchill followed up with an encouraging letter, urging the university to stay the course. Elon's third application was approved at the Triennial Council in Austin, Texas, on October 2, 2009.

In my estimation, the importance of Phi Beta Kappa to Elon cannot be overstated, and its presence continues to profoundly influence the campus. The pursuit of a Phi Beta Kappa chapter was instrumental in forming Elon's identity as a liberal arts university committed to preparing each student with the foundational knowledge and skills necessary for success as twenty-first-century global citizens. Every undergraduate benefited from expanded library collections, an improved student-faculty ratio, and investments in faculty. Majors and minors in the arts and sciences have also increased; today, half of Elon undergraduates earn a major in an arts and sciences discipline and more than two-thirds major or minor in the arts and sciences.

The faculty and staff who are members of the Eta chapter at Elon meet regularly and seek to advance the university in important ways. Notably, an office of national and international fellowships has been formed at Elon to encourage students to apply for the Rhodes, Marshall, Mitchell, Goldwater, Truman, Fulbright, and other prestigious awards for graduate study. While no Elon student has yet been named a Rhodes Scholar, Elon students have won Goldwater, Mitchell, Udall, and Truman scholarships, and Elon has been named one of the most productive campuses for the Fulbright scholarship.

The story of Elon's pursuit of a Phi Beta Kappa chapter

is one of leadership and persistence. Russ Gill, Distinguished University Professor and Maude Sharpe Powell Professor of English; Helen Walton, instructor of mathematics; and Steven House, then-dean of Elon College, the College of Arts and Sciences, and professor of biology provided strong leadership of this initiative for a decade. Gill, Walton, and House were confident that their plans and recommended investments in arts and sciences were making the university noticeably stronger year by year. The mantra, "The journey is more important than the destination," was often repeated during that decade.

The seven-building Academic Village was completed in 2013, providing a second prominent campus quadrangle dedicated to the arts and sciences. The quad is anchored by the Martha S. and Carl H. Lindner III Hall, which houses several arts and sciences departments and programs and the Office of the Dean of Elon College. I recall Mr. Lindner telling me that he became intrigued with the Elon story and business model after reading *Transforming a College*. The Lindners later made a lead gift to fund one of the university's top capital priorities, another example of parent leadership and generosity that has advanced Elon.

Two other prominent programs in the Academic Village are the Belk Pavilion, housing the Center for the Advancement of Teaching and Learning, and the Numen Lumen Pavilion, Elon's new multi-faith center. Both are situated symbolically at the center of campus.

The Flourishing of Professional Schools

Elon is a liberal arts university, blending the best of a strong liberal arts and sciences tradition with opportunities for professional study for undergraduates in the Martha and Spencer Love School of Business, the School of Communications, and the School of Education. At the graduate and professional levels, a School of Law and a School of Health Sciences have been established since the original publication of *Transforming a College*. Each of the professional schools has achieved significant national recognition that George Keller foreshadowed. Today, Elon University is one of only seven private institutions of higher education to shelter a chapter of Phi Beta Kappa and host an AACSB-accredited business school, an ACEJMC-accredited communications school, an ABA-accredited law school, and an NCATE-accredited education school. (The other six institutions are American, Baylor, Columbia, Hofstra, Marquette, and Syracuse.) Programs in the School of Health Sciences also hold their highest respective accreditations.

As with the pursuit of a chapter of Phi Beta Kappa, the accreditation of the professional schools led to focused investments in academic quality, especially in the number of new faculty lines, which brought incredible intellectual energy and new levels of scholarly achievement to campus. Investments in faculty scholarship, facilities, technology, and student scholarships were also spurred by accreditation standards and goals.

A handsome new home for the Love School of Business, designed by Spillman-Farmer Architects, was realized in 2006 with the completion of the Ernest A. Koury Sr. Business Center. With a new building in place and the accreditation efforts completed, two deans have worked in succession with the faculty to advance the Love School. During Dean Mary Gowan's tenure, three new academic centers were established with generous gifts from trustees: the Doherty Center for Entrepreneurial Leadership, the Chandler Family Professional Sales Center, and the Porter Family Professional Development Center. Professorships were also endowed by the Elingburg family and the Love Family Foundation. The twenty-fifth anniversary of the school was celebrated in 2011. The Doherty and Chandler centers brought distinctive new programmatic strengths to students in the Love School and ushered in an era at Elon when academic deans would become much more active in fund raising for their respective schools.

Especially with a heightened emphasis on securing good internship and job placements for business graduates, the national profile of the Love School has risen substantially since George Keller's last visit to Elon. The Elon Commitment strategic planning process envisioned a top-50 *Bloomberg Businessweek* ranking for the Love School, which was unranked when the plan was conceived in 2009. It is now ranked #42 nationally, and the part-time MBA program holds the #5 ranking in its category by *Bloomberg Businessweek*. In 2012 Dean Raghu Tadepalli was recruited from Babson College to lead the school's future development. Dean Tadepalli is now leading an important conversation about expanding the school's graduate programs. The Love School enrolls sixteen hundred undergraduate majors.

Dean Paul Parsons remains at the helm of the School of Communications and has led the school through a decade of accomplishment, including the growth of the faculty from eleven to forty-eight today. In 2011–12 the ACEJMC accreditation site team reported that "the growth of the School—in quality and quantity—is nothing short of spectacular. And it has been an integral and respected part of an institution whose standing also has skyrocketed . . . This is a university clearly on the move—as is the School." Dean Parsons was selected by the Scripps Howard Foundation as administrator of the year and presented an award at the meetings of the Association for Education in Journalism and Mass Communications in 2011. Indeed, the School of Communications has become a "lighthouse" academic program for Elon, with a strong emphasis on field-based work.

The School of Communications has added a master of arts in interactive media, along with the Elon in LA (Los Angeles) summer and semester-long programs, giving Elon an important West Coast presence for internships, student recruiting, and alumni networking. Significantly, the school hosts the Imagining the Internet Center, which sends student-faculty teams abroad each year to cover Internet forums and technology conferences, tracks predications about how the Internet is changing our world, and partners on research projects with the Pew Internet & American Life Project. The Imagining the Internet Center has allowed the School of Communications to claim a position of international expertise in a rapidly changing field and provides students with a vision for the future of communications—a unique advantage in launching their careers.

Student accomplishments in the School of Communications have been nationally recognized. Recent awards include the College Television Award for best student television newscast, the nation's #1 collegiate television journalist in the Hearst Journalism Awards, and the winner of the Sprite Films competition in both the judge's award and popular vote, a work inspired by a London street scene the filmmaker saw while on study abroad.

Afterword
119

When George Keller was writing this book, Elon was considering a feasibility study for a school of law—one that Keller found "questionable." Following a two-year study, the board of trustees voted to establish the Elon University School of Law in downtown Greensboro, North Carolina, approximately twenty miles from the main campus. Jim Melvin, president of the Joseph M. Bryan Foundation, was instrumental in marshaling the philanthropic leadership of the Greensboro community to commit $10 million in start-up funding as well as provide a facility for the new school, a former Greensboro public library building that underwent a complete renovation under the direction of Shepley Bulfinch architects.

The new school was dedicated on September 19, 2006, by Associate Justice of the United States Supreme Court (retired) Sandra Day O'Connor. From the outset, the school has aimed to be "a law school with a difference," seeking to set an innovative path for legal education at Elon. Hallmarks of the school include its preceptor program, in which each new student is assigned a practicing attorney as a mentor, and its leadership development program, which won the E. Smythe Gambrell Professionalism Award from the American Bar Association in 2013. In 2012, the School of Law was named one of the nation's most innovative law schools by the *National Jurist*. The school received both initial accreditation and full accreditation by the American Bar Association at the earliest possible opportunity and is planning to seek membership in the American Association of Law Schools. A graduate of the Elon Law charter class, David Morrow, received the Junius W. Williams Young Lawyer of the Year Award from the National Bar Association in 2013.

Nonetheless, much hard work remains to fully establish the school. The great recession of the past decade substantially reduced the demand for new lawyers, and applications to U.S. law schools have declined approximately 50 percent, two factors unimagined in the feasibility study. In this environment, it is critically important to continue to define the special character and curricular and programmatic strengths of the young law school.

As the NewCentury@Elon strategic plan was drawing to a close, Provost Steven House appointed a faculty committee to study the establishment of a School of Health Sciences to respond to growing demands for health-care providers, especially in the area of primary care. While the existing doctoral program in physical therapy would naturally be housed in the new school, serious consideration was given to additional graduate programs in the health professions, including physician assistant studies and pharmacy. After much study, the physician assistant (PA) studies program was selected for development, as the need for physician extenders is expected to grow tremendously as a result of health-care reform and concerns about access and cost. Dr. Elizabeth Rogers, former chair of the Department of Physical Therapy, was named dean of the new school. The first class of students in the new PA program was seated in January 2013.

To house the new school, the university purchased nine acres of land abutting the east edge of campus and a 150,000-square-foot building (with a Georgian façade nicely matching the architecture of the campus) from Smithfield Foods Company in 2010. The transformation of a building from a country ham processing plant to a School of Health Sciences took imagination and money and ranks as one of the university's greatest recycling and reuse projects. The renovated facility was named in honor of Gerald L. Francis, former provost and current executive vice president, in recognition of his decades of exemplary service to Elon as an administrator and faculty member.

Each of the professional schools is supported by an active and thoughtful advisory board comprising alumni, parents, and friends of Elon. NBC News anchor Brian Williams, a parent of a 2013 alumnus, and David Gergen, former advisor to four U.S. presidents, chair the communications and law school advisory boards, respectively.

The Transformation of the Residential Campus

At a time when many have predicted that the bricks and mortar campus is a dinosaur, Elon is doubling down on its commitment to enhance the residential nature of its 620-acre campus. A key initiative of the Elon Commitment strategic plan, Elon is aiming to have more faculty and staff in residence, create more living-learning communities, and further enhance the intellectual climate on campus through the residential experience. Many of the best universities in the United States are residential campuses, and the experience students gain through living in community with others is central to an Elon education.

Four major new residential complexes have opened since 2004 and three older complexes have been demolished. The new residential neighborhoods include the Oaks, a seven-building apartment-style complex; the Colonnades, a six-building residential quad that includes a dining hall and geothermal heating and cooling; the Station at Mill Point for juniors and seniors, a grouping of twenty-four buildings reminiscent of Charleston architecture oriented toward a central courtyard with career advisors in residence; and the Global Neighborhood, an internationally themed 600-bed complex that includes a 30,000-square-foot commons building housing the Isabella Cannon Global Education Center, classrooms, faculty offices, faculty-in-residence, and a great hall seating 1,500 people.

The Faculty Teacher-Scholar-Mentor Model

George Keller wondered how Elon would balance the tensions in its changing identity—for example, maintaining an active, engaged style of teaching and learning while producing impressive faculty scholarship. Teaching remains the clear top priority in evaluating faculty work at Elon; tenure and promotion are dependent on a demonstrated record of excellence and commitment as a teacher. At the same time, expectations for faculty scholarship have risen and in fact have been driven by faculty members committed to their scholarship and understanding that scholarship and teaching are mutually reinforcing and inseparable professional activities. In 2008 a report of the Presidential Task Force on Scholarship was completed under the leadership of Distinguished University Professor Tom Henricks and Professor Tim Peeples, now associate provost. The report spurred a $6 million base-budget investment in release time to support faculty scholarship, new funds for sabbaticals and summer support, and broader celebration of faculty scholarship on campus, including many new faculty awards for scholarly excellence. The authors found that there is no "old" or "new" Elon, but rather a university that "is distinguished by its ongoing commitment to institutional change" and the ability to "build itself anew" every year in response to new challenges.

Elon faculty members continue to blend teaching and scholarship by mentoring student undergraduate research. Elon's students are very well represented at the annual National Conference on Undergraduate Research, as well as scholarly conferences nationally and internationally. In 2007 the Lumen Prize was created, providing $15,000 awards annually to fifteen sophomores who craft ambitious plans for research and creative activities to be carried out during their junior and senior years under the guidance of experienced faculty research mentors.

The Deepening of Experiential Learning Programs

For the past several years, *U.S. News & World Report* has recognized institutions that do an exemplary job with high-impact learning in a ranking titled "A Focus on Student Success." There are eight categories: first-year experiences, internships/co-ops, senior capstone experiences, undergraduate research/creative projects, learning communities, study abroad, service learning, and writing in the disciplines. Elon is the only school in the nation to be listed among the leading schools in seven of the eight categories; the next most-represented institutions in 2014 were Stanford University (five categories) and Duke University and Carleton College (four categories).

Elon has continued to invest heavily in the quality of its signature experiential learning programs, believing that this is now central to its institutional identity and to its demonstrated track record of student retention and success after college. As examples, the university won the Senator Paul Simon Award for campus internationalization in 2007 and recently committed to quadruple need-based aid to encourage every undergraduate to participate in a study abroad or Study USA program. In 2006 President George W. Bush presented Elon with the inaugural President's Community Service Honor Roll Award, a recognition that has been repeated annually. The Elon Experiences (study abroad, internships, undergraduate research, leadership, and service) remain among the university's most important programs, and students often cite them as a principal reason for choosing Elon. Despite George Keller's worry that Elon would have trouble balancing Phi Beta Kappa quality academics and experiential learning, experience has shown that academics and experiential learning have blossomed in complementary ways.

Financial Basics

George Keller would find most of the financial basics being practiced at Elon in 2004 still adhered to today. The university steadfastly maintains its low tuition discount rate of about 15–16 percent. To achieve greater socioeconomic diversity in the student body, Elon has relied on annual fund raising and endowment returns for new need-based scholarships, rather than elevating the discount rate. We continue to remain convinced that institutional discount rates in the 40–60 percent range are unsustainable in the long run.

Elon's tuition, room, board, and fees crossed the $40,000 threshold for the 2013–14 academic year, still a relative value in the private college and university marketplace. The university is committed to protecting its value as a competitive advantage, and thus for the past several years Elon has kept annual tuition increases under 4 percent. This means that discretionary dollars for new initiatives funded through tuition are competitively awarded, especially given the university's commitment to the advancement of faculty and staff salaries relative to peer and aspirant institutions. The university issued salary raises each year during the financial crisis and the subsequent recession and furloughed no employees, recognizing that its people were its most important asset for students.

The university has continued to assume a greater debt load to support construction of revenue-producing facilities such as residence halls and dining halls. No debt has been issued in the past fifteen years for construction or renovation of academic or athletics facilities; those projects have been funded through a combination of fund raising and institutional expenditures.

Elon remains true to the board of trustees mandate to avoid deferred maintenance. Each summer the university invests millions of dollars in roof replacements, parking lot resurfacing, energy efficiency projects, and general repairs and refurbishments, a strategy that avoids crushing repair costs down the road. From my first year at Elon, students often have remarked, "As soon as I got out of the car on my first visit, I knew this was where I was going to school." And while they are referring, in part, to the manicured campus, I believe prospective students and parents make an inferential leap—that if they take such good care of the campus, care must be displayed in other ways as well. And that is true.

In 2008, under the leadership of Dr. James Powell, then board chair, and Gerald Whittington, senior vice president for business, finance, and technology, Elon adopted an outsourced chief investment officer strategy, liquidating all of its endowment assets and reinvesting them with Global Endowment Management of Charlotte, North Carolina. This strategy has allowed Elon to pursue more diversified, high-quality, and well-researched investments than it would have had access to if managing its own funds. In a stroke of good timing, Whittington completed the liquidation of endowment assets into cash just prior to the great crash of 2008, saving the university millions of dollars.

Elon's Weaknesses and the Making of Turnarounds

Every institution has challenges and weaknesses, and we are lucky—we have friends who will kindly help us discover and correct them. Two examples from Elon's recent past are illustrative, and both have significant strategic importance.

Several years ago, parents began saying to me, "No institution does a better job acculturating first-year students to the university. You do a great job on the front end, but you are less effective in supporting students' success following graduation." They were right. Our students were continually getting better and they had higher expectations for their careers, but the economy was in free fall and jobs were scarce. Parents were telling me that the placement of students upon graduation was a key component of institutional value.

Under the leadership of Associate Provost Constance Ledoux Book, Elon's approach to career services was totally reinvented to serve the needs of students who come to career services for help in achieving a specific goal, such as "I want to work in finance in New York" or "I want to serve in the Peace Corps." Book made a great hire in Tom Brinkley as executive director of employer relations. Brinkley partnered with deans, parents, alumni, and friends of the university to develop a much more robust network of potential employers. Next, a beautiful new Student Professional Development Center (SPDC), funded by parents, was located in the Moseley Student Center, where students would walk by it every day. Finally, with the SPDC as the hub, Elon invested in satellite career and internship advising in the undergraduate professional schools and in Elon College, the College of Arts and Sciences. From their first day on campus, students learn that a successful career takes planning and that internships are key to launching careers, providing invaluable real-world experience and a network of contacts. We have also been busy promoting the Elon Network, an idea that originated with students. We stress that everyone is a part of the Elon Network—alumni, parents, students, friends—and that we each have a responsibility to help students and alumni advance in their careers.

We have seen similar advances in student acceptances to some of the nation's best graduate and professional schools, including Yale School of Drama, Harvard Medical School, Chicago and Berkeley law schools, and top Ph.D. and master's programs, as well as enhanced success in students receiving national and international fellowships.

Another arena in which Elon was falling behind was alumni relations. With a remarkably young alumni body, Elon needed to seize the opportunity to encourage these alumni to become engaged, lifetime advocates for their university. After all, the most measurable and visible learning outcome of our work at Elon, as with any university, is the success of its alumni.

A multi-part plan to advance alumni relations was developed. The Martin Alumni Center opened in the heart of the historic campus, a refurbished former private home that provides a place of welcome for returning alumni. At the MAC, alumni can see an alumni video produced by two recent graduates of the School of Communications, learn about how they can reengage with campus, and embark on a campus tour. Several new alumni engagement officers were added to the staff, reinforcing the message that Elon needs its alumni to be engaged with the university on many fronts: sharing their expertise in the classroom, advocating for Elon alumni in securing internships and employment, supporting Phoenix athletics, speaking to prospective students about Elon, and, of course, making financial contributions every year to support current and future students. New plans are being formulated to expand programming for alumni—on campus, through active chapters across the United States, and via technology—to keep graduates engaged with the intellectual life of campus, professional development opportunities, and Phoenix athletics.

A More Diverse Campus

Stemming from a conviction that it is essential to cultivate intercultural competence for a twenty-first-century world for each of our students, the university set important goals with regard to diversity and global engagement in the Elon Commitment strategic plan. Multicultural enrollment has grown from 12.2 percent of the first-year class in 2004 to 17.3 percent in 2013. This growth has been principally fueled by a commitment to double need-based aid for lower- and middle-income families in this decade. Major new need-based scholarship programs have been established to augment the successful Watson Scholarship referenced by George Keller, including a $5 million gift from alumnus Furman Moseley to endow the Susan Scholarships, in honor of his wife Susan Moseley, to support women of promise with limited financial means. Today 17 percent of Elon faculty members are from diverse racial and ethnic backgrounds, ahead of many of our peer and aspirant institutions.

While historically affiliated with the United Church of Christ and continuing to focus on its mission to nourish the mind, body, and spirit, the university has responded to a growing religious diversity in its student body, including many who describe themselves as "spiritual" or "seeking" but not religious. A multi-faith center, the Numen Lumen Pavilion, opened in 2013 in the heart of campus—a sign to students from all faiths and spiritual traditions that they are welcome on campus and an acknowledgment that greater religious understanding is central to peace in the world today. The Sklut Hillel Center, which opened in 2013, and a Roman Catholic Newman Center also serve two of Elon's fastest-growing religious groups on campus, each with full-time staff and vibrant programming, alongside longstanding groups such as the Intervarsity Christian Fellowship and a new part-time Muslim chaplain.

A new Gender & LGBTQIA Center is housed in the student center, along with identity spaces to support Elon's African American, Hispanic/Latino/a, and Asian students. The financial investments required to achieve these aspirations are significant but essential to preparing young people for leadership in an increasingly diverse society.

Elon is also striving to triple international enrollment. Progress is being achieved on this front, but not as rapidly as we hope—a not uncommon situation for institutions that are still working to earn international reputations. A goal has been set to provide 100 percent access to an international or Study USA experience by dramatically increasing need-based aid for this purpose. We expect that participation rates in these programs will rise from the current 72 percent to approach 90 percent by 2020. In the Ever Elon campaign, forty-seven new endowments were created to support study abroad scholarships.

Elon has made important commitments to local K-12 education to serve the community in which faculty and staff and their families reside. The university created the Elon Academy in 2007 to support talented students in six local high schools who come from families with no history of college attendance and of modest financial means. Directed by Professor Deborah Long, the Elon Academy offers a three-week, residential program on campus in the summer following the scholars' freshman, sophomore, and junior years, including courses taught by Elon faculty and visits to colleges and universities. Saturday enrichment sessions, parental involvement, and intensive mentoring and counseling have led to a very high rate of acceptances into colleges and universities, with several full scholarships, including three Gates Millennium Scholars. The program is fully funded by private philanthropy, especially by Elon alumni. In many important ways, the Elon Academy has nurtured the soul of Elon University.

The Village Project, directed by Professor Jean Rattigan-Rohr with support from the Oak Foundation, provides individualized instruction for struggling readers and their families, as well as enrichment programs in math, science, and music. The Village Project, the Elon Academy, and new need-based scholarships form a strong foundation for an emphasis at Elon today on college access and success.

Interim Associate Provost Brooke Barnett has provided outstanding leadership in this area of campus life, chairing Elon's Inclusive Community Council. She has also worked diligently to put systems into place across human resources, student life, academic affairs, and other areas to make Elon a more welcoming, fair, and inclusive place.

Phoenix Athletics

Athletics Director Dave Blank has provided exemplary leadership of the department since the retirement of Dr. Alan White in 2006. Thirty-six teams or individuals have won Division I Southern Conference championships since Elon joined the conference in 2003, and the department claims 20 All-American honorees, 10 SoCon players of the year, and 11 SoCon freshmen of the year; 735 student-athletes have earned Academic All-Conference Honors.

Facilities additions include Alumni Field House at the north end of Rhodes Stadium, Hunt Softball Park, and Worsley Golf Center, with extensive renovations and improvements to Alumni Gymnasium, Koury Field House, Powell Tennis Center, and Latham Baseball Park. Seventeen sports are offered at Elon today—seven men's teams and ten women's teams, with the latest addition being women's lacrosse.

In 2013, Elon accepted an invitation to join the Colonial Athletic Association beginning in 2014. This new conference aligns well with Elon undergraduate recruiting and alumni demographics, with schools located in four of the nation's largest media markets. While coaches and athletes are excited about a high level of competitive play, the move better aligns the institution with its natural geographic footprint.

The Changing Business Model for Higher Education

In the age of Massive Open Online Courses and the proliferation of online degree programs, as well as blended and flipped classrooms, this would be a fascinating time to have George Keller visit Elon again to opine about how technology will change our future. Mark London, a prominent Washington attorney and a member of Elon's School of Law Advisory Board, recently introduced me to Brian Kelley, editor of *U.S. News & World Report.* Mr. Kelley predicted that a large number of U.S. colleges will close or merge in the years ahead, unable to attract sufficient enrollment, keep up with aging infrastructures, or compete with low-cost online options. For those skeptical of his prediction, he offers this reminder: "We used to print a magazine."

There are certainly many threats to higher education ahead. The iceberg of college costs is real, and increasingly we hear the public say they are not willing to pay higher costs. Another threat is the environment of declining state and federal support and increasing government regulation for public and private higher education. I am sure that some colleges and universities will not survive the convergence of these storms.

The world of online learning continues to shape higher education, including at Elon, where our summer school has principally migrated to online courses, benefiting students who wish to pursue internships or employment and continue to take classes. Forty-four such classes were offered in the summer of 2013.

Provost Steven House has recently written a white paper for campus discussion to help us discern Elon's place in the world of online, hybrid, flipped, and blended classes, indeed an essential conversation for residential campuses enrolling students who have had every dimension of their lives shaped by technology.

Going forward, I have confidence about the future of institutions such as Elon, even in the throes of huge technological change, because of the following principles.

1. The residentially based college and university that provides a strong liberal arts and sciences foundation for a lifetime of learning is going to continue to matter *if* institutions pay attention to a high-quality undergraduate experience offering quality teaching and mentoring and transforming experiential education. We must keep in mind that we are not in the business of offering classes; we are in the business of human transformation. The challenge is to make this deeply enriching and transforming style of education accessible to more families who cannot afford the full cost of attendance.

2. Both sticker price and net costs matter to families. The days of ramping up tuition 6–8 percent annually to fund institutional ambitions are over. Prospective students and families will seek value, which speaks to price, overall quality, and outcomes after college.

3. Institutional brand will matter more than ever. Institutions with national brands will continue to thrive, while those with regional brands will be more vulnerable. Elon's national and increasingly international reach for students is a key aspect of a stable future for us.

4. Outcomes after college will matter more than ever—universities must demonstrate impact. Families investing $150,000 or more in an education will demand more information about opportunities for access to high-quality graduate programs and gainful and meaningful employment.

5. Institutions that fail to innovate and reinvent themselves continuously are at risk of ossification. I recall a recent conversation with a fellow college president whose board had authorized the addition of graduate programs; three years later, the faculty had finally approved a short definition of what a graduate program was. The world is changing at a fast pace around us, and failure to adapt will be perilous.

6. A quality faculty and staff are the best resource we offer students. We can never lose sight of this. Another college president visiting Elon recently walked the campus for some time before joining me in my office for lunch. He reported he had talked to fifty people, all of whom were friendly, offered assistance, and were obviously proud of their institution. He told me, "You can't bottle that." When I talk to seniors and alumni about their Elon experiences, the conversation inevitably turns to the faculty and staff who changed their lives through meaningful and deep personal relationships. The quality of these relationships remains at the heart of an academic community.

Afterword

Dan Currell, a thoughtful trustee at Gustavus Adolphus College, recently reflected on the challenges facing colleges in a column for *Inside Higher Ed*, titled "What Is College For?" He noted that with a growing number of low-cost educational options, colleges must answer a key question: "Since there are now innumerable other (and cheaper) ways to be educated, why are we doing *this*?"

"The colleges with a compelling answer to that question—where all 3,000 people know the answer—are going to be fine . . . Deciding on a clear and important set of goals will not be easy, but colleges cannot afford to kick that can down the road. We each need to figure out what *our* college is for," Currell wrote.

We continue to refine our answer to that very basic and compelling question—still searching for the cool spot on the pillow—even with the bedrock support for the core mission of Elon affirmed by students, faculty, staff, alumni, parents, trustees, and friends. If we discern our future together, avoid complacency, embrace innovation, and stay true to our closely held values, there will undoubtedly be more exciting chapters to write. I thank you for your interest in Elon's story and hope that, in some small way, George Keller's telling of that story has helped you to reflect on your institution's path to a higher level of excellence.

Leo M. Lambert

ACKNOWLEDGMENTS

My interest in Elon College, as it was then called, began in August 1996, when President Fred Young asked me to visit the campus for a small consulting assignment. I became fascinated with what Elon College was doing and how it was doing it. I subsequently returned to the college for interviews and document reading and then wrote an article about Elon in the Spring 1997 issue of *Planning for Higher Education*.

In September 2002 President Leo Lambert, Young's successor, called to inquire whether I would be available for a second consulting assignment: producing an update of the 1997 article. After meeting with many of the principals and several faculty in October, I proposed that I write a small book about Elon's climb from mediocrity and poverty to distinction in the past half-century. Dr. Lambert agreed, and he promised—and gave—complete editorial freedom as well as full cooperation in providing data, interviews with his colleagues, and his own personal views.

I wanted to write this book for two reasons. One was to describe how a private American college can transform itself using strategic planning, financial ingenuity, faculty dedication, and strong, determined leadership. The other reason was to fill a curious void in the literature and scholarship about U.S. higher education.

There exist numerous institutional histories celebrating achievements, what one of my manuscript's referees called "vanity histories." And there are hundreds of statistical analyses, models, descriptions of particular areas of university operations (such as admissions procedures, research activity, arrangements for minorities, athletic programs), as well as numerous pronouncements about the state of higher learning, in the current scholarship and appraisals of colleges and universities. But with very few exceptions, such as Morton and Phyllis Keller's (no relation) *Making Harvard Modern: The Rise of America's University* (2001), American scholars of higher education have seldom ventured to study in detail a single institution's policies, plans, people, and progress. Micro studies to investigate how one college or university conducts itself are extremely rare.

My debt to the trustees, administrators, faculty, students, and some parents of Elon University is huge. Without their unfailing candor and assistance, I would not have been able to understand the anatomy and actions of this institution.

Presidents Fred Young and Leo Lambert have both been uncommonly frank and supportive. I also want to thank especially Jacqueline Wehmueller, the extraordinary executive editor at the Johns Hopkins University Press, and my wife, Jane, whose long devotion is matched by her own scholarly attentions.

INDEX

Academic Council, 2, 5
academic programs, 2, 57–75;
plans for, 65–71; restructuring,
62–65; Young (J. Fred) and,
9–10, 14, 16–21, 27. *See also*
faculty
Academic Village, 46, 67–68, 71,
72, 94, 116
accreditation of professional
schools, 117
adjunct instructors, 80
admissions, 94, 101; diversity
in, 129–30; increase in, 29,
84, 113; investment in, 78;
Lambert (Leo) and, 43–45, 72;
Young (J. Fred) and, 12–14
Advanced Institutional Development Program (AIDP), 9–10
African American students, 5,
46, 88, 91
Agnes Scott College, 22, 67
Allen, Noel, 31, 65, 69
alumni giving, 16, 34–35, 80,
86
alumni relations, 128–29
Anderson, Dan, 47, 104, 105, 109
Asian students, 91
Associated New American Colleges (ANAC), 63, 64

Association of American Colleges and Universities, 64–65
Association to Advance Collegiate Schools of Business
(AACSB), 73
athletic scholarships, 38, 91–92
athletics program, 20, 37–40,
132–33

band, marching, 37
Barner, Jack, 34
baseball park, 38
Belk Library, 3, 26, 27, 29, 58,
62, 66
Berry College, 3
Blank, Dave, 132
Bloomquist, Rich, 95
Board, Warren, 15
board of trustees. *See* trustees
Book, Constance Ledoux, 127
Boyer, Ernest, 63
Brinkley, Tom, 128
Bromilow, Neil, 24, 37
budget, 2, 10, 24, 82–84
buildings: construction of new,
2–3, 14, 27, 29, 67, 69, 79, 99;
renovation of, 3, 14, 67
Burbridge, John, 73
Bush, George W., 125

139

business model for higher
education, 133–36
business office, 22–24
business school, 14, 62, 63, 68,
69, 71, 73, 117–18

Calhoun, Michael, 15–16, 20
campus beauty, 2, 8–9, 14, 24,
25, 79, 99, 126
career planning, 10, 50, 127–28
Catawba College, 7
celebrations, 48–50
Chandler, Wallace, 26, 60, 76
chorus, a capella, 49
citizen surveys, 49–50
cleanliness, 24, 25, 99. *See also*
campus beauty
Coca-Cola, "pouring rights" of, 81
cocurricular program, 2, 20–21,
50
Communication, Department of,
61, 62
Communications, School of, 63,
69, 71, 73–74, 118–19
community sense, 1, 3, 41,
100–102
competition, xv, xvi–xvii, 7, 113
computer system, 22, 66, 77
construction, new, 2–3, 14, 27,
29, 67, 69, 79, 99
consultants, 25, 104
Cooperative Institutional
Research Project (CIRP), 52
co-op students, 21, 50
corporate gifts, 34, 85, 86
Council of Independent Colleges,
30
counseling, 10, 44
"critical thinking" workshops, 15
Currell, Dan, 136
curriculum. *See* academic
programs

D'Amato, Richard, 61
Danieley, James Earl, 4–6, 33,
100, 110
Danieley Center, 46
Davidson College, 3, 13
debt, 5, 16, 79–80, 126
deferred gifts, 10, 34, 85
Dillashaw, F. Gerald, 73
diversity, 91, 129–32
dormitories, 10, 24
Drew, Gail, 32–33
Duke Science Building, 14

East Gym, 38
Education, Department of, 62
Education, School of, 14, 63, 73
El Centro de Español, 62
Elite Program, 49
Ellerbe Becket, 36
Elon 101, 42–43
Elon Academy, 131, 132
Elon Athletic Foundation, 40
"Elon Bubble," 53–54, 91–92,
101
Elon Commitment, 111–12, 118,
122, 129–30
Elon Experiences, 2, 20–21, 50,
102, 125
Elon Home for Children, 87
Elon Magazine, 7–8
Elon Medallion, 110
Elon Network, 128
Elon University Poll, 49–50, 105
Elon Vision, 26–28, 29, 30, 65,
66, 84
endowment, 3; under Danieley
(James Earl), 5; growth of, 112;
outsourced chief investment
officer strategy, 127; under
Smith (Leon Edgar), 4; Whit-
tington (Gerald) and, 22–23,
27, 77, 78, 81–82; under Young

(J. Fred), 6, 13, 22–23, 27–28,
    77–78
engaged learning, 50–52, 55, 102
engineering, 61
enrollment, 3–4, 5, 6–7, 9, 10, 13,
    78, 90–91, 113
Enterprise Academy, 49
ethnic diversity, 91, 129–30
Ever Elon campaign, 112–13
experiential learning programs,
    124–25
extroverts, 18–19

faculty: diversity of, 130; expecta-
    tions for, 92–93; full-time, 111;
    growth of, 80; hiring of, 15–16,
    29, 59–61, 62, 73, 101; impor-
    tance of, 135; as introverts, 19;
    orientation for, 60; sabbaticals
    for, 61; salaries of, 27, 29,
    58, 77, 80, 82, 85, 101, 126;
    scholarships of, 57–58, 59–60;
    as skeptical of changes, 17–18,
    99–100; student-centered,
    41, 102; as student sponsors,
    48; studying abroad, 62;
    teacher-scholar-mentor model,
    123–24; wellness education
    campaign for, 23; workload of,
    16, 58; young, 15, 29, 89
Faculty Administrative Fellows
    program, 110
Fellows Competition Weekend,
    42
fellowships, 42, 93
field, athletic, 36–37, 38
Fighting Christians, 10, 39, 40
finances, 76–87, 103–4, 125–27;
    and budget, 2, 10, 24, 82–84;
    and debt, 5, 16, 79–80; Young
    (Fred) and, 6–7, 9, 27, 77–78.
    See also endowment; fund

raising; gift(s); tuition; Whit-
    tington, Gerald
financial aid, 23, 84–85, 91
fine arts building, 14
fitness facility, 3, 20
Fonville Fountain, 14, 28
food, 2, 23–24
football team, 10
foreign students, 47
foundations, gifts from, 34, 86
founding of college, 4
fountain, 14, 28
Francis, Gerald, 101; and aca-
    demic programs, 17–18, 19,
    20; and ANAC membership,
    63, 64; and athletic pro-
    gram, 39; and budget, 83; as
    executive vice president, 109;
    and financial aid, 23; hiring
    new faculty, 59–60; Lambert
    (Leo) and, 33; and library, 26;
    on scholarships of faculty, 60;
    School of Health Sciences and,
    121–22
fraternity houses, 3, 46
Frontani, Heidi Glaesel, 61
fund raising, 10, 16–17, 26, 27,
    29, 40, 69, 85–86
Furman University, 3

Gaff, Gerry, 25
Gardner, John, 43, 89
Gergen, David, 122
gift(s): from alumni, 16, 34–35,
    80, 86; from corporations,
    34, 85, 86; deferred, 10, 34,
    85; from foundations, 34, 86;
    from parents, 34, 36, 80, 86
Gill, Russell, 17, 62, 72, 94,
    116
Gordon, Barbara, 15
government loan, 10

Gowan, Mary, 117–18
graduate programs, 14
grant, 9, 10, 11, 23, 57
grounds crew, 24–25
guidance counselors, 44
Guilford College, 7, 13
gymnasium, 38

Habitat for Humanity, 21
Harrigan, Dan, 67
Harris, Nancy, 58
Harvard Schmarvard (Mathews),
    89
Hazel, Michael, 50
health plan, 23, 86
Health Sciences, School of,
    121–22
Hendricks, Thomas, 62, 123
Hispanic students, 91
Holland House, 34
honors students: fellowships
    for, 93; pavilion for, 46–47,
    72; program for, 71, 85, 93;
    scholarships for, 71–72
Hood, Richard, 41
House, Steven, 74, 109, 116,
    121, 134
housing, student, 3, 10, 14, 24,
    45–47, 72

Imagining the Internet Center,
    119
Institutional Self-study for the
    Southern Association of Col-
    leges and Schools, 90
Institutions of Excellence in the
    First College Year, 43
instructors, adjunct, 80
insurance, medical, 23
internships, 20, 21, 50, 102
Isabella Cannon International
    Studies Pavilion, 46

Isabella Cannon Leadership
    Program, 21, 51

Jackson, Smith, 21, 27, 47, 49,
    82, 101, 109
Jewish students, 91
Jimmy Powell Tennis Center, 14
job offers to graduates, 94–95
Jordan Center, 68

Keller, George, xi, 109
Kelley, Brian, 133
Kernodle Center for Service
    Learning, 50
Klopman, Susan, 34, 44–45, 101,
    110
Koury Business School, 68
Koury Center, 3, 14, 20, 38
Kuh, George, 54–55

Lambert, Leo Michael: and
    Academic Village, 46, 94;
    and admissions, 43–45; and
    ANAC membership, 63, 64;
    and athletics program, 37, 38;
    and budget, 83; hiring new
    faculty, 59–60; introduction to
    college of, 33; land purchase
    by, 86–87; Leadership Elon
    sessions by, 95; and marching
    band, 37; and marketing, 104,
    105; and multicultural recruit-
    ment, 91; and Parents Council,
    36; personnel changes by,
    33–34; planning by, 65–66, 68,
    71; restructuring by, 62–65;
    salary of, 81–82; and scholar-
    ships of faculty, 57–58, 59; and
    scholarships of students, 72,
    85, 91; selection as president
    of, 32, 101; and study abroad
    program, 51

Latham Baseball Park, 38
law school, 70, 71, 120–21
leadership: strategic planning
    and, 111–12; of trustees, 112–13;
    in vice-presidential roles, 110
Leadership Elon sessions, 95,
    100
leadership opportunities, 21, 51
learning: engaged, 50–52, 55,
    102; experiential learning pro-
    grams, 124–25; service, 21, 50
Learning Resource Center, 10
Lewis Clarke Associates, 8
liberal arts education, 63–65, 71,
    93–94, 97, 115, 116–17, 134
library. *See* Belk Library
Life Stories (course), 48–49, 102
Lindner, Carl H. and Martha S.,
    116
living-learning centers, 46
loan, government, 10
location of college, 11–12, 80
London, Mark, 133
Long, Deborah, 131

magazine, 7–8
Magoon, Michael, 34
Maher, Julianne, 1, 28, 33–34, 59
maintenance, 2, 24–26, 99, 126.
    See also campus beauty
marketing, 11–12, 104–5
Martha and Spencer Love School
    of Business, 14, 62, 63, 69, 71,
    73, 117–18
Martin Alumni Center, 129
McBride, A. Wayne, Jr., 8–9, 25
McBride, Rev. Richard, 28, 48,
    49, 82, 101, 102, 110
McEwen Building, 73–74
McKinnon Field, 36–37
McMichael Science Center, 3, 58
McNeela, Catherine, 60–61

medical insurance plan, 23
Melvin, Jim, 120
Meredith, Joseph, 61
Moncure, James, 7–8
Moore, Keith, 25
Morrow, David, 120
Moseley Center, 3, 20
MSG (Male Singing Group), 49
music, 49, 61
Myers, Clair, 15
Myers-Briggs Type Indicator test,
    18–19

name change: from Elon College
    to Elon University, 2, 63;
    from Fighting Christians to
    Phoenix, 39
National Association of Educa-
    tion Buyers, 82
National Association of Intercol-
    legiate Athletics (NAIA), 10, 38
National Collegiate Athletic Asso-
    ciation (NCAA), 38
National Conference on Under-
    graduate Research, 52
National Survey of Student
    Engagement (NSSE), 55, 88
NewCentury@Elon, 68–71, 95,
    111, 121
North Carolina Teaching Fellows
    program, 73

Office of Institutional Advance-
    ment, 85
Olmsted, Frederick Law, 8
open houses, 44
orientation: faculty, 60; student,
    42–43
out-of-state enrollment, 113

parents, 35–36; campus beauty
    praised by, 25; gifts from, 34,

parents (*continued*)
36, 80, 86; incomes of, 78;
suggestions by, 52–53; support
of, 113; tuition payment by, 79
Parents Council, 35–36, 52–53
Parsons, Paul, 74, 118, 119
pavilion, honor student, 46–47
Peeples, Tim, 123
Perkins, Nan, 11, 34, 44, 78, 85,
86, 101, 110
Peterson, Sara, 33
Phi Beta Kappa chapter, 70, 71,
72, 94, 114–16
Phoenix, 39–40
Phoenix Card, 81
physical therapy, 61
Piatt, Jim, 109
"Plan for the 90s," 16–21
planning, 26, 27, 65–71, 99–100
Policy Center on the First Year of
College, 43, 52, 89
Poulson, Linda, 61
Powell, James, 126–27
Powell, Maude Sharpe, 116
professional schools, 116–22
promotional materials, 44, 47,
104–5
proprietary colleges, 16
prospective students, 42, 44–45

quality, institutional, 22–26,
98–99

Rattigan-Rohr, Jean, 132
recognition of college, 3, 44,
54–56, 88–89, 105
Reichard, Rosalind, 58
Reilly, Annie, 95
religious diversity, 130
renovation, building, 3, 14, 67
repositioning of college, 10,
12–13, 35

research, 52
residence halls, 14, 46–47,
122–23
retention rate, 43
retreat, 42
Rhodes Stadium, 36–37
Rich, Lela Faye, 18, 52, 101, 110
Rogers, Elizabeth, 61, 121
running track, 3, 38
Ruth, Mary, 35, 36

sabbaticals, 61
salaries, faculty, 27, 29, 58, 77,
80, 82, 85, 101, 126
Sanford, Michael, 15
Sarwi, Cindy Wall, 35
scholarships, 57–60, 74–75,
78, 79, 85, 92–93; athletic,
38, 91–92; honors, 71–72;
for low-income students, 91;
needs-based, 125, 130, 132
science building, 3, 14, 27, 29,
58
Senior Satisfaction Surveys, 2,
52
service learning, 21, 50
service recognition luncheons,
110–11
Seven Lakes Retreat, 42
singing groups, a capella, 49
Skube, Michael, 61
Smith, Leon Edgar, 4
softball field, 38
sorority houses, 3, 46
Southern Association of Colleges
and Schools (SACS), 70, 90
Spanish language, 62
Spencer Love Foundation, 11
Spillman, Robert, 67, 68, 71
Spillman Farmer (firm), 67–68
spiritual growth, 48–49
Spray, Sharon, 49, 105

Springer, Robert, 53
stadium, 3, 27, 29, 36–37
staff: full-time, 111; importance
  of, 135
Stein, Jeffrey, 47, 82
strategic planning, 111–12. *See
  also* Elon Commitment
Strempek, Barth, 49
student counseling, 10
student-faculty ratio, 111
student growth, 57, 92, 102
student housing, 3, 10, 14, 24,
  45–47, 72
student life, 41–56; celebrations
  and involvements, 48–50;
  engaged learning, 50–52, 55,
  102; in freshman year, 42–43;
  Young (Fred) and, 7–8, 9
Student Professional Development Center, 128
students, 3–4; African American, 5, 46, 88, 91; Asian, 91;
  birthdays of, 48; co-op, 21, 50;
  diversity of, 129–32; on "Elon
  Bubble," 53–54; as extroverts,
  18–19; faculty sponsors of,
  48; foreign, 47; Hispanic, 91;
  honors (see honors students);
  Jewish, 91; job offers to, 94–
  95; orientation for, 42–43;
  prospective, 42, 44–45; retention rate of, 43; suggestions of,
  49; surveys of, 52–53. *See also*
  admissions
student surveys, 52–53
study abroad program, 19, 20,
  51, 62, 81
success, reasons for, xii–xiv
Sullivan, John, 62, 110
survey: citizen, 49–50; student,
  2, 52–53, 55, 88
Sweet Signatures, 49

Tadepalli, Raghu, 118
teacher-scholar-mentor model,
  123–24
teaching workshops, 15
technology, 66, 90
Technology Center, 66
tennis center, 14
therapy, physical, 61
Tinto, Vincent, 25
track, running, 3, 38
trees, 25
trustees, 6, 9, 12–14, 26, 31–32,
  78, 80–81, 83–84, 112–13
tuition, 6, 9, 13, 23, 45, 78, 79,
  84–85, 103, 125–26, 134
"Turning 21" ceremony, 48
Twisted Measure, 49

Undergraduate Research Forum,
  58
United Church of Christ, 7, 11, 33
University of Wisconsin–La
  Crosse, 31–32
U.S. News & World Report, 3, 88,
  114, 124, 133

Village Project, 132
"The Voices of Discovery" (lectures), 58, 105
volunteer service, 21, 50

Web site, 47
wellness course, 20, 102
wellness education campaign, 23
White, Alan, 12, 37, 38, 39, 101,
  110, 132
Whittington, Gerald, 76–87,
  101, 103, 109, 126–27; on Belk
  Library, 26; and budget, 24,
  82–84; cost-saving efforts of,
  80–81; course taught by, 82;
  and debt, 79–80; on "Elon

Whittington, Gerald (*continued*) way," 100–101; and endowment, 22–23, 27, 77, 78, 81–82; and financial aid, 23; and food, 23–24; on hiring faculty, 62; Spillman Farmer hired by, 67; and tuition, 78, 79, 84–85; under Young (Fred), 77–78
Williams, Brian, 122
Williams, Jo Watts, 5–6, 16, 33
Wilson, Edwin, 63
Wong, Frank, 63–65
Wright, Dan, 71
Writing Program, 15

Young, J. Fred: and academic programs, 9–10, 14, 16–21, 27; and athletics program, 37; and campus beauty, 8–9, 14, 79; and Elon Experiences, 20–21; and finances, 6–7, 9, 27, 77–78; and financial aid, 23; land purchase by, 8; and marketing, 104; praise for, 25–26, 101; and quality, 22–26, 98–99; retirement of, 29–31, 110; and student life, 7–8, 9; and study abroad program, 51
Yow-Bowden, Deborah, 39–40

Zaiser, Greg, 109–10
Z. Smith Reynolds Foundation, 10